PRENTICE HALL SCIENCE

Activity Book

EXPLORING PLANET EARTH

Prentice Hall
Englewood Cliffs, New Jersey
Needham, Massachusetts

Activity Book

PRENTICE HALL SCIENCE
Exploring Planet Earth

ISBN 0-13-400615-1

  4 5 6 7 8 9 10   97 96 95

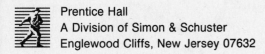
Prentice Hall
A Division of Simon & Schuster
Englewood Cliffs, New Jersey 07632

Contents

To the Teacher

The materials in the *Activity Book* are designed to assist you in teaching the *Prentice Hall Science* program. These materials will be especially helpful to you in accommodating a wide range of student ability levels. In particular, the activities have been designed to reinforce and extend a variety of science skills and to encourage critical thinking, problem solving, and discovery learning. The highly visual format of many activities heightens student interest and enthusiasm.

All the materials in the *Activity Book* have been developed to facilitate student comprehension of, and interest in, science. Pages intended for student use may be made into overhead transparencies and masters or used as photocopy originals. The reproducible format allows you to have these items easily available in the quantity you need. All appropriate answers to questions and activities are found at the end of each section in a convenient Answer Key.

CHAPTER MATERIALS

In order to stimulate and increase student interest, the *Activity Book* includes a wide variety of activities and worksheets. All the activities and worksheets are correlated to individual chapters in the student textbook.

Table of Contents

Each set of chapter materials begins with a Table of Contents that lists every component for the chapter and the page number on which it begins. The Table of Contents also lists the number of the page on which the Answer Key for the chapter activities and worksheets begins. In addition, the Table of Contents page for each chapter has a shaded bar running along the edge of the page. This shading will enable you to easily spot where a new set of chapter materials begins.

Whenever an activity might be considered a problem-solving or discovery-learning activity, it is so marked on the Contents page. In addition, each activity that can be used for cooperative-learning groups has an asterisk beside it on the Contents page.

First in the chapter materials is a Chapter Discovery. The Chapter Discovery is best used prior to students reading the chapter. It will enable students to discover for themselves some of the scientific concepts discussed within the chapter. Because of their highly visual design, simplicity, and hands-on approach to discovery learning, the Discovery Activities are particularly appropriate for ESL students in a cooperative-learning setting.

Chapter Activities

Chapter activities are especially visual, often asking students to draw conclusions from diagrams, graphs, tables, and other forms of data. Many chapter activities enable the student to employ problem-solving and critical-thinking skills. Others allow the student to utilize a discovery-learning approach to the topics covered in the chapter. In addition, most chapter activities are appropriate for cooperative-learning groups.

Laboratory Investigation Worksheet

Each chapter of the textbook contains a full-page Laboratory Investigation. A Laboratory Investigation worksheet in each set of chapter materials repeats the textbook Laboratory Investigation and provides formatted space for writing observations and conclusions. Students are aided by a formatted worksheet, and teachers can easily evaluate and grade students' results and progress. Answers to the Laboratory Investigation are provided in the Answer Key following the chapter materials, as well as in the Annotated Teacher's Edition of the textbook.

Answer Key

At the end of each set of chapter materials is an Answer Key for all activities and worksheets in the chapter.

SCIENCE READING SKILLS

Each textbook in *Prentice Hall Science* includes a special feature called the Science Gazette. Each gazette contains three articles.

The first article in every Science Gazette—called Adventures in Science—describes a particular discovery, innovation, or field of research of a scientist or group of scientists. Some of the scientists profiled in Adventures in Science are well known; others are not yet famous but have made significant contributions to the world of science. These articles provide students with firsthand knowledge about how scientists work and think, and give some insight into the scientists' personal lives as well.

Issues in Science is the second article in every gazette. This article provides a nonbiased description of a specific area of science in which various members of the scientific community or the population at large hold diverging opinions. Issues in Science articles introduce students to some of the "controversies" raging in science at the present time. While many of these issues are debated strictly in scientific terms, others involve social issues that pertain to science as well.

The third article in every Science Gazette is called Futures in Science. The setting of each Futures in Science article is some 15 to 150 years in the future and describes some of the advances people may encounter as science progresses through the years. However, these articles cannot be considered "science fiction," as they are all extrapolations of current scientific research.

The Science Gazette articles can be powerful motivators in developing an interest in science. However, they have been written with a second purpose in mind. These articles can be used as science readers. As such, they will both reinforce and enrich your students' ability to read scientific material. In order to better assess the science reading skills of your students, this *Activity Book* contains a variety of science reading activities based on the gazette articles. Each gazette article has an activity that can be distributed to students in order to evaluate their science reading skills.

There are a variety of science reading skills included in this *Activity Book*. These skills include Finding the Main Idea, Previewing, Critical Reading, Making Predictions, Outlining, Using Context Clues, and Making Inferences. These basic study skills are essential in understanding the content of all subject matter, and they can be particularly useful in the comprehension of science materials. Mastering such study skills can help students to study, learn new vocabulary terms, and understand information found in their textbooks.

ACTIVITY BANK

A special feature called the Activity Bank ends each textbook in *Prentice Hall Science*. The Activity Bank is a compilation of hands-on activities designed to reinforce and extend the science concepts developed in the textbook. Each activity that appears in the Activity Bank section of the textbook is reproduced here as a worksheet with space for recording observations and conclusions. Also included are additional activities in the form of worksheets. An Answer Key for all the activities is given. The Activity Bank activities provide opportunities to meet the diverse abilities and interests of students; to encourage problem solving, critical thinking, and discovery learning; to involve students more actively in the learning experience; and to address the need for ESL strategies and cooperative learning.

Contents

*Appropriate for cooperative learning

Chapter Discovery   **Earth's Atmosphere**

Plants and the Atmosphere

Background Information

In photosynthesis, green plants use sunlight, water, and carbon dioxide gas to make food. During this process, plants break down water molecules into hydrogen and oxygen atoms. In this activity you will find out how the process of photosynthesis affects the composition of the Earth's atmosphere.

Problem

How do plants affect the composition of the Earth's atmosphere?

Materials

2 small *Elodea* plants (you can buy these at a pet supply store)
2 wide-mouthed jars
2 glass funnels
2 test tubes
2 wooden splints
lighter

Procedure

1. In the bottom of each wide-mouthed jar, place an *Elodea* plant.

2. Fill each jar about half full with water.

3. Place a funnel over each plant, top side down.

4. Fill a test tube with water. Hold your thumb over the open end of the tube to keep the water from spilling. Turn the test tube upside down. Then lower the test tube under the water in one of the jars and over the stem of the funnel.

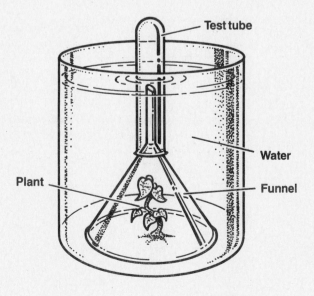

© Prentice-Hall, Inc.

5. Repeat step 3 for the other jar.

6. Place one jar in the sun. Place the other jar in a dark place.

7. Wait 24 hours.

8. Carefully remove the test tube from the jar that was in the sun. As you do so, keep your thumb over the test tube opening.

9. Use the lighter to light one of the wooden splints. **CAUTION:** *Always be careful when working with an open flame.*

10. Blow out the flame. Very quickly, while the splint is still glowing, remove your thumb from the opening and plunge the glowing splint into the test tube. What happens to the splint?

_____

11. Repeat steps 8 through 10 with the test tube from the jar that was in the dark. What happens to the splint?

_____

Critical Thinking and Application

1. What factor was different for the two *Elodea* plants in this experiment? _____

_____

_____

_____

2. What happened to the glowing splint when it was placed in the test tube that was over the plant kept in sunlight? _____

_____

_____

_____

3. What gas must have been present in this test tube? Why? _____

_____

_____

_____

4. How do you account for the presence of this gas? _____

_____

_____

_____

_____

5. Was the same gas present in the test tube that was over the plant kept in the dark?

How do you account for this? _____

_____

_____

_____

6. Based on this experiment, what gas is released into the atmosphere by green plants?

Why is this gas important? _____

_____

_____

_____

7. How do green plants contribute to the constant composition of the Earth's

atmosphere? _____

_____

_____

_____

_____

Activity

Earth's Atmosphere

It's Getting Colder

The temperature of the troposphere decreases an average of 6.5°C for every kilometer above the Earth's surface. If the surface temperature on a hot summer day is 35°C, what is the temperature of the air at each kilometer above the surface up to a height of 12 km? Write your answers in the chart.

Kilometer(s) Above the Earth's Surface	Temperature
1	
2	
3	
4	
5	
6	
7	
8	
9	
10	
11	
12	

Activity _____

Examining Temperature Patterns in the Atmosphere

If it were possible to climb up a ladder through the atmosphere and measure the air temperature as you traveled, you would discover the pattern of atmospheric temperatures shown in the graph. This graph shows how the atmosphere is divided into four distinct temperature zones that are separated from one another by a series of boundaries referred to as "pauses."

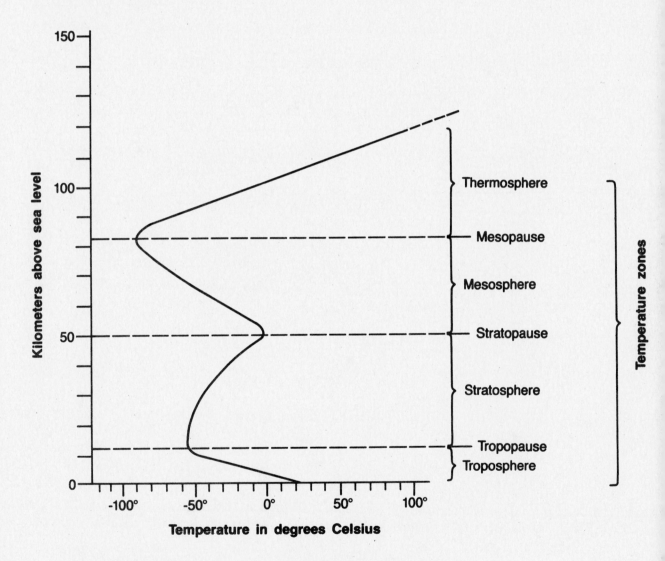

Refer to the graph to answer the following questions.

1. a. Which of the four temperature zones is the thinnest? _____

b. Approximately how thick is it? _____

2. How thick is the stratosphere? _____

3. How thick is the mesosphere? _____

4. Which temperature zone do we live in? _____

5. As you move upward through the troposphere, what happens to the temperature of the atmosphere? _____

6. a. What is the approximate temperature of the atmosphere at the stratopause?

_____

b. What is the approximate temperature of the atmosphere at the Earth's surface (sea level)? _____

c. At what approximate height above sea level does the graph indicate the temperature of the atmosphere is the coldest? _____

7. In which temperature zones does the atmospheric temperature increase as the distance above sea level increases? _____

8. Describe the change that occurs in the pattern of atmospheric temperatures at the "pauses." _____

_____

Land, Water, and Air Temperature Changes

You may have noticed that on a hot summer day, the sand at the beach is often uncomfortably hot, while the water seems cool to the touch as you wade in. If you have ever gone swimming in the evening or early in the morning, you may also have noticed that the reverse seems to be true. The water at those times seems to be warmer than the sand. Temperature differences such as these are not imaginary; they are real and not at all unusual. In fact, observations made with thermometers placed in the air above the water and sand will verify that the air, as well, is cooler above the water during the day and warmer above the water at night. Additionally, careful observation of air movement above the land and water surfaces reveals the existence of convective circulation: warm air rising above the sand in the day with cooler air sinking over the water. This type of air circulation is sometimes referred to as a land or sea breeze. Land breezes occur during the night and sea breezes occur during the day.

In this activity you will be given some information and data about a laboratory setup designed to help you study land and water temperature changes as land and water are heated and cooled by the process of radiation.

The diagram on the right illustrates a laboratory activity that was set up to compare temperature changes of dry soil and water surfaces that were warmed by radiation from a heat source. The containers were heated for 10 minutes and then allowed to cool for 10 minutes following the removal of the energy source. A thermometer was placed in each container so that the bulbs were just beneath the surface of the material. The heat source was positioned so that it was the same distance from each container. Temperature readings were recorded each minute during both the heating and cooling periods. The results of the investigation are contained in the Data Table.

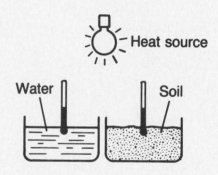

Heat source

Water   Soil

DATA TABLE

Lamp On (Heating Period)

Time (min)		0	1	2	3	4	5	6	7	8	9	10
Temperature (°C)	Soil	20.0	21.0	22.0	23.0	24.0	26.0	27.0	28.5	30.0	31.0	32.0
	Water	20.0	20.5	21.0	21.5	22.0	22.0	22.5	22.5	23.0	23.0	23.0

Lamp Off (Cooling Period)

Time (min)		11	12	13	14	15	16	17	18	19	20
Temperature (°C)	Soil	32.0	31.0	30.5	29.5	28.0	27.0	26.0	25.0	23.5	22.0
	Water	22.5	22.5	22.0	22.0	22.0	21.5	21.5	21.0	21.0	20.5

Using the information in the Data Table, construct a graph on the grid provided. Your graph should show the relationship between temperature changes and time for the materials in both containers. Plot a single curve for each substance.

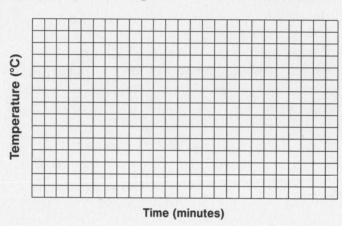

Time (minutes)

Questions

1. Which surface received more energy from the heat source, the soil or the water?

   _____

2. a. Which surface heated more quickly, the soil or the water?

   _____

   b. Which surface cooled more quickly, the soil or the water?

   _____

3. Do you think the soil would have heated differently if it had been moist rather than

   dry? _____

   Explain your answer. _____

   _____

   _____

4. Do you think the water would have heated differently if it had been muddy rather

   than clear? _____ Explain your answer. _____

   _____

   _____

5. Refer to the diagram on the right. In what direction would you expect air to be moving above the containers at the end of the 10-minute heating period? Using arrows, make a rough sketch to illustrate the direction of air movement under such conditions.

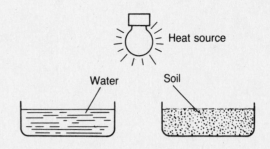

6. In general, what effects do differences in heating and cooling rates of land and water surfaces have upon the temperature and motion characteristics of air directly above them?

_____

_____

_____

Activity

Plotting Radio Reception

To find out from how far away radio waves can be received during the day and night, try the following. Listen to an AM radio during the day and late at night. Record the number of stations you can receive during the day and at night. Note their locations. Using the space below, plot the stations on a map.

1. Which of the radio stations you were able to receive during the day was the farthest

   away? _____

   At night? _____

2. Why do you think the number of stations you could receive during the day was

   different from the number of stations you could receive at night? _____

   _____

   _____

   _____

   _____

Activity

Global Wind Patterns

The Earth's surface is constantly being heated by energy from the sun. Because tropical regions are warmed more effectively than polar regions, differences in atmospheric pressure develop between these latitude extremes. Such pressure differences result in planetwide winds.

Air heated at the surface in the lower latitudes is lifted and replaced by cooler, denser air flowing from the higher latitudes. If the Earth did not rotate, if it were not inclined on its axis, and if the surface were uniform throughout, planetary atmospheric circulation would probably be relatively simple. Alas, such is not the case! In fact, global wind systems are extremely complex and details of worldwide wind patterns are still not clearly understood by scientists. However, basic circulation patterns do exist that are recognized by scientists and are used to help understand certain worldwide climate and weather patterns.

The purpose of this activity is to examine the location and extent of some of the general planetary wind and pressure systems that are currently recognized. In order to complete this activity, you will need to keep three facts in mind:

A. Air tends to flow out of regions characterized by relative high pressure and into regions characterized by relative low pressure.

B. Because of the Earth's rotation, winds tend to be deflected or directed toward the right in the northern hemisphere, and toward the left in the southern hemisphere.

C. Winds are named for the direction from which they originate. For example, a northerly wind is one that flows from the north.

Now refer to Figure 1 on page 24, which represents a rough sketch of the Earth. Note that the locations of the equator (latitude zero), the poles (latitude 90°), and latitudes 30° and 60° have been identified. Additional information will be added to the map as you complete this activity.

Pressure Belts and Planetary Winds

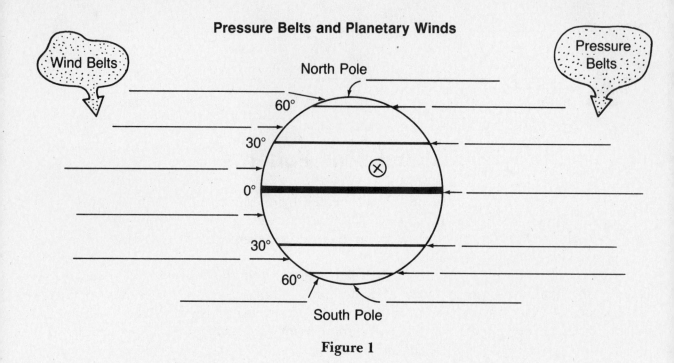

Figure 1

On the right side of Figure 1 and in the appropriate space provided, label each of the seven pressure belts. The equator is a low pressure belt and is referred to as the Equatorial Low. Latitudes 30° north and south are high pressure zones and are each referred to as a Subtropical High. Latitudes 60° north and south are low pressure belts and are each known as a Subpolar Low. Finally, the polar regions are high pressure zones and each should be labeled as a Polar High.

In the proper location, sketch in the direction of planetary wind movement within each global wind belt. Use several arrows in each zone to illustrate the direction of deflection, as shown in the following key. Be sure to place directional arrows, right on the map, within all six wind belt regions.

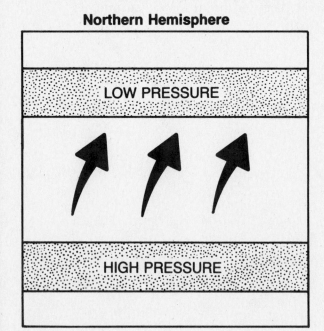

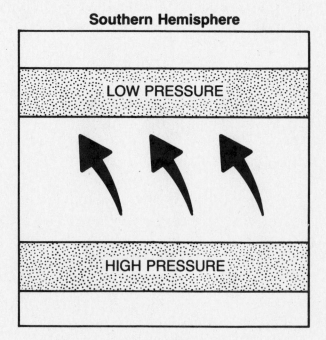

On the left side of Figure 1 and in the appropriate space provided, label the names of the wind belts. Remember winds are named for the direction from which they flow. Winds located between latitudes zero and 30° are known as Trade winds. Thus, if winds within this zone originated in the northeast, they would be known as Northeast Trades. Winds located between latitudes 30° and 60° are referred to and named by the direction from which they have originated. They are further described as prevailing winds. Thus, if winds within these zones originated in the northwest, they would be referred to as Prevailing Northwesterlies. Winds located between latitudes 60° and 90° (the North or South poles) are referred to as Polar winds. Therefore, winds located in these zones, which originate in the east, are known as Polar Easterlies.

Questions

1. What causes winds to be deflected to the right or left as they flow from high

   pressure to low pressure? _____

2. Name the wind belt in which you live. _____

3. Name the prevailing winds that would be found at location X (refer to Figure 1).

   _____

   _____

4. Why is air pressure generally lower over equatorial regions than over polar regions?

   _____

   _____

Activity _____ Earth's Atmosphere

Temperature and Pressure Patterns in the Troposphere

The atmosphere extends outward into space for several thousand kilometers from the Earth's surface. However, the bottom 10 kilometers of the atmosphere make up the most important layer for the people who live on the Earth. This layer, called the troposphere, is where the weather occurs that has such a great effect on our lives.

In this activity you will construct graphs that reveal the temperature and pressure patterns that exist in the troposphere.

Use the temperature data to construct a graph that shows how the average air temperature of the atmosphere changes as you move upward in the troposphere, away from the Earth's surface.

Use the atmospheric pressure data to construct a graph that shows how the average atmospheric pressure changes as you move upward in the troposphere, away from the Earth's surface.

Height Above Earth's Surface (in meters)	Average Atmospheric Pressure (in millibars)	Average Air Temperature (in °C)
0 (sea level)	1013.2	15.0
500	954.6	11.8
1000	898.8	8.5
1500	845.6	5.2
2000	795.0	2.0
2500	746.9	− 1.2
3000	701.2	− 4.5
3500	657.8	− 7.7
4000	616.6	−11.0
4500	577.5	−14.2
5000	540.5	−17.5
5500	505.4	−20.7
6000	472.2	−24.0
6500	440.8	−27.2
7000	411.0	−30.4
7500	383.0	−33.7
8000	356.5	−36.9
8500	331.5	−40.2
9000	308.0	−43.4
9500	285.8	−46.7
10,000	265.0	−49.9

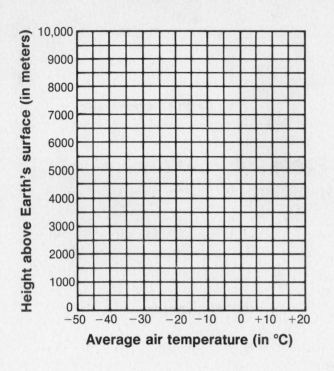

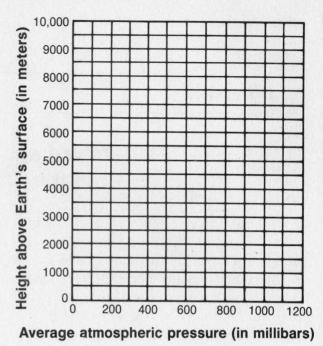

Questions

1. Describe the way in which air temperature changes as you move upward in the troposphere, away from the Earth's surface. _____

   _____

   _____

   _____

2. Describe the way in which the atmospheric pressure changes as you move upward in the troposphere, away from the Earth's surface. _____

   _____

   _____

   _____

Activity

CHAPTER

Earth's Atmosphere

1

Composition of the Atmosphere: A Graphic Model

The Earth's atmosphere is made up of a mixture of gases, liquids, and solids. However, the largest part, by far, consists of those substances that are usually found as gases. One exception, of course, is water. Water is nearly always present in the atmosphere as a liquid, solid, or gas. When it exists as a vapor, the amount of water in the "air" varies considerably from place to place and time to time. Variation may be as much as 3 percent. Most of the gases that make up the rest of the atmosphere are found in amounts nearly unchanging in any particular location or at any given height above sea level.

In this activity you will construct a series of bar graphs that illustrate the relative amounts of those gases that make up more than 99 percent of the nonchanging components of the Earth's atmosphere.

Examine the Data Table from the American Meteorological Society. This table lists by volume, the percentage amounts of the four gases that make up most of the Earth's atmosphere.

DATA TABLE

Gases	Volume by Percentage
Argon	0.93
Carbon dioxide	0.03
Nitrogen	78.08
Oxygen	20.95

Total = 99.99

Using the information provided in the Data Table and the graph paper included with this activity, construct a graph that consists of four separate bar graphs, one graph for each of the atmospheric components listed. You may color in each of the graphs using the colors of your choice. Label each column and indicate the percentage of gas in each column.

After completing the four bar graphs, answer the following questions.

1. a. Which is the most abundant gas found in the Earth's atmosphere? What is its

   percentage? _____

   b. List in order of abundance from most to least, the four major components of the

   Earth's atmosphere. _____

2. What is the probable reason for the fact that water vapor was not included in the Data Table of the major atmospheric components, even though it is often present in amounts far greater than either argon or carbon dioxide?

_____

_____

_____

3. What percentage of the volume of the Earth's atmosphere is not accounted for in

the data provided? _____

4. Find information in a textbook about weather or the atmosphere at least five atmospheric gases other than those graphed in the activity. Indicate percentage to which they are present. What is the total percentage of the gases you listed? How does this total compare to any one of the gases you graphed?

_____

_____

_____

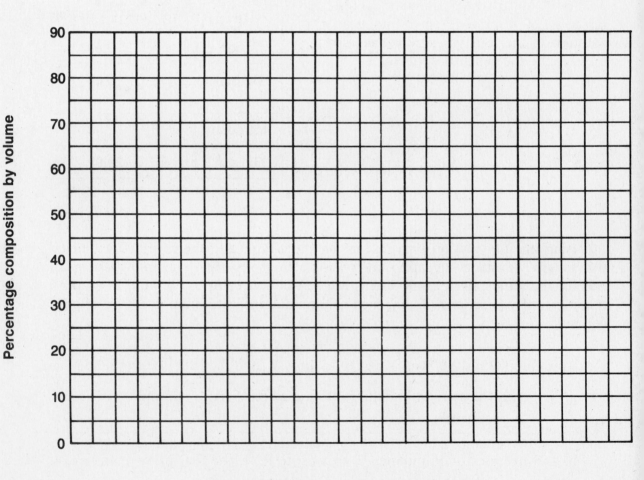

Major components of Earth's atmosphere

_____ *Laboratory Investigation* _____

CHAPTER 1 ■ Earth's Atmosphere

Radiant Energy and Surface Temperature

Problem
Does the type of surface affect the amount of heat absorbed both in and out of direct sunlight?

Materials *(per group)*
10 thermometers
stopwatch or clock with sweep second hand
2 shallow containers of water

Procedure 🔺
1. Place a thermometer on the grass in the sun. Place a second thermometer on the grass in the shade.
2. Place two of the remaining thermometers—one in the sun and one in the shade—on bare soil, on concrete, on a blacktop surface, and in water.
3. After 2 minutes, record the temperature of each surface.
4. Continue recording the temperature of each surface every 2 minutes for a period of 10 minutes.
5. Record your results in a data table similar to the one shown here.

Surface	Temperature in the Sun					Temperature in the Shade				
	2 min	4 min	6 min	8 min	10 min	2 min	4 min	6 min	8 min	10 min
Grass										
Soil										
Concrete										
Blacktop										
Water										

Observations
1. Which surface was the warmest? Which surface was the coolest?

_____

_____

2. By how many degrees did the temperature of each surface in direct sunlight change during the 10-minute time period? _____

_____

_____

3. By how many degrees did the temperature of each surface in the shade change during the 10-minute period? _____

_____

_____

Analysis and Conclusions

1. Why do you think the warmest surface was the warmest? _____

_____

_____

2. How do you explain the temperature change that occurred in water? _____

_____

_____

3. What conclusions can you reach about the amount of heat energy different surfaces absorb from the sun? _____

_____

_____

_____

4. On Your Own   How can you apply your observations to the kinds of clothing that should be worn in a warm climate? In a cold climate? In what other ways do the results of this investigation affect people's lives?

Answer Key

Chapter Discovery: Plants and the Atmosphere

Procedure   10. The splint bursts into flame.   **11.** The flame goes out.   **Critical Thinking and Application   1.** One was placed in the sun, the other was kept in the dark.   **2.** The splint burst into flame. **3.** Oxygen. Oxygen is needed in order for things to burn.   **4.** The *Elodea* plant was carrying out photosynthesis while it was in the light. Oxygen, produced during photosynthesis, was released into the test tube.   **5.** No. Plants do not undergo photosynthesis in the absence of light. **6.** Oxygen. This gas is needed by humans and other animals for respiration. **7.** Green plants continually replenish the Earth's supply of oxygen. Plants also use up the carbon dioxide produced by other organisms during respiration.

Problem-Solving Activity: It's Getting Colder

1 km 28.5°C   **2 km** 22.0°C   **3 km** 15.5°C **4 km** 9.0°C   **5 km** 2.5°C   **6 km** −4.0°C **7 km** −10.5°C   **8 km** −17.0°C **9 km** −23.5°C   **10 km** −30.0°C **11 km** −36.5°C **12 km** −43.0°C

Activity: Examining Temperature Patterns in the Atmosphere

1. a. Troposphere   b. 12–13 km   **2.** 37–38 km   **3.** 32–33 km   **4.** Troposphere **5.** Temperature decreases   **6.** a. 0°C b. 20°C   c. At the mesopause or approximately 82–83 km above sea level.   **7.** In the stratosphere and in the thermosphere.   **8.** As you move up in the atmosphere, the pattern of temperature changes reverses at the "pauses."

Discovery Activity: Land, Water, and Air Temperature Changes

Check graphs to make sure that they accurately reflect the information in the Data Table.   **1.** Both containers received the same amount of energy. The soil absorbed it more quickly.   **2.**   a. soil (darker, rougher, lower specific heat)   b. soil (A good absorber of energy is a good radiator of energy.)   **3.** Yes. Moisture would cause the soil to heat more slowly.   **4.** Yes. Due to the darkening effect of the soil in the water, it would have heated more quickly.   **5.** Air will be moving from the heat source to the water, to the soil, to the atmosphere. Diagrams should reflect this.   **6.** The more quickly the surface heats, the more quickly the air above it will heat. The warmer the air, the less dense it becomes. Thus, it will rise. Conversely, cooler air will tend to sink over cooler surfaces.

Problem-Solving Activity: Plotting Radio Reception

1. Students should discover that radio stations received during the day were all within 200 km of their radio. At night, depending on atmospheric conditions, students should have picked up stations up to 1000 km away. Because the ionosphere is higher at night, radio signals are bounced greater distances off it.   **2.** For this reason, the number of stations received at night is greater than the number received during the day.

Activity: Global Wind Patterns

Figure 1 north to south   **Pressure belts** polar high, subpolar low, subtropical high, equatorial low, subtropical high, subpolar low, polar high   **Planetary wind movements** southwest, northeast, southwest, northwest, southeast, northwest   **Wind belts** Polar Easterlies, Prevailing Southwesterlies, Northeast Trades, Southeast Trades, Prevailing Northwesterlies, Polar Easterlies   **Questions   1.** the rotation of the Earth from west to east, producing the so-called Coriolis effect   **2.** Answers will vary.   **3.** Northeast Trades   **4.** Tropical regions are warmed more effectively than are higher latitudes. As a result, average air temperature is higher, producing lower atmospheric pressure.

Problem-Solving Activity: Temperature and Pressure Patterns in the Troposphere

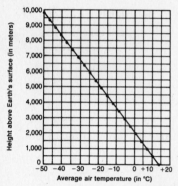

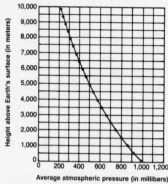

graphed, especially nitrogen, oxygen, and argon.

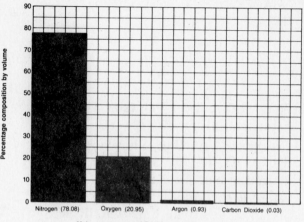

Major components of Earth's atmosphere

Questions   1. As height above the Earth's surface increases, the average temperature of the air decreases.   **2.** As height above the Earth's surface increases, the average atmospheric pressure decreases.

Activity: Composition of the Atmosphere: A Graphic Model

1. a. Nitrogen (78.08 percent)   b. Nitrogen, oxygen, argon, carbon dioxide   **2.** It is one of the highly variable atmospheric components. Variation can range from 0 percent to about 3 percent.   **3.** 0.01 percent   **4.** Neon (Ne) 0.00182 percent (This percentage and the following percentages are all approximations.)   Helium (He) 0.00053 percent   Krypton (Kr) 0.00012 percent   Xenon (Xe) 0.00009 percent   Hydrogen (H_2) 0.00005 percent   Methane (CH_3) 0.00002 percent   Nitrous oxide (N_2O) 0.00005 percent   Total of 0.00268   The total percentage will vary but will be about 0.003 percent. Total is far less than any of the gases

Laboratory Investigation: Radiant Energy and Surface Temperature

Observations   1. Students should find that temperatures in the sun are higher than those in the shade. They should observe that the blacktop has the highest temperature, followed by the concrete, soil, grass, and water.   **2.** Students should observe that temperature change was rapid on the blacktop, concrete, and soil. The grass would also show a slight temperature change but not as great as the previous three surfaces. Very little temperature change will be noted in the shallow pan of water because the sun's heat energy is more slowly absorbed by the water than by the other surfaces.   **3.** Students should observe that all surfaces had similar temperature changes.   **Analysis and Conclusions   1.** The blacktop absorbs more heat energy from the sun because the color black is a poor reflector of heat energy. **2.** The sun's heat energy is more slowly absorbed by the water than by the other surfaces.   **3.** Dark surfaces, such as blacktop and possibly soil, absorb more radiant energy than lighter surfaces do.   **4.** Light-colored clothing should be worn in warm climates and dark-colored clothing in cold climates. One possible application of the investigation is in heating buildings. Homes that have a black roof would absorb more radiant energy from the sun than would homes with a light-colored roof. Therefore, energy consumption in these homes would be greater during the summer when air conditioning is used to cool the home.

Contents

*Appropriate for cooperative learning

CHAPTER 2

Chapter Discovery

Earth's Oceans

Help! I'm Drowning

Background Information

Would you rather drown in salt water or fresh water? Of course, this is a really silly question. Drowning is drowning, no matter what type of water you drown in. But suppose the question were stated differently: "Imagine that you are in danger of drowning. Would you rather be in fresh water or salt water?" Keep this question in mind as you carry out this activity.

Materials

pen with waterproof ink
ruler
masking tape
scissors
glass container (about 2 L)
spoon or stirring rod
modeling clay
plastic drinking straw
table salt
balance

Procedure

1. Cut a piece of masking tape about 10 cm long. Make a line down the center of the tape about 8 cm long. Make a metric scale on the tape by placing marks 1 mm apart. Make the first line and every fifth line longer. Number your scale in intervals of five.

2. Attach the tape to the straw so that the zero end of the scale is even with the end of the straw.

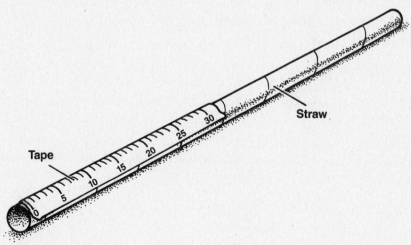

3. Make a ball of clay about 2 cm in diameter. Push the clay into the end of the straw away from the zero end of the scale.

4. Fill the glass container about half full with water. Place the straw in the water vertically with the clay end down, as shown. The straw should float. If it does not, make the clay ball larger or smaller.

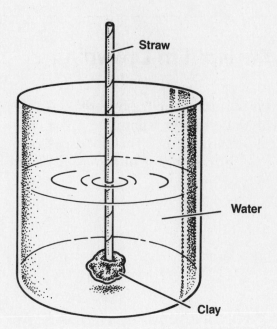

5. Note where the surface of the water touches the metric scale. Record the number

from the scale here: _____

6. Remove the straw from the water. Use the balance scale to measure 10 g of table salt.

7. Stir the salt into the water. Place the straw back in the water.

8. Note where the surface of the water touches the metric scale. Record the number

here: _____

9. Remove the straw from the water. Measure out 10 g more of table salt and stir it into the water. Now you have a total of 20 g of salt in the water.

10. Place the straw back in the water. Where does the surface of the water touch the

metric scale? Record the number here: _____

11. Repeat steps 9 and 10 two more times. Record below where the surface of the water touches the metric scale.

30 g: _____

40 g: _____

Critical Thinking and Application

1. How did the position of the straw change as you added more salt to the water?

   _____

   _____

2. What does this tell you about the way objects float in salt water compared with the way objects float in fresh water?

   _____

   _____

3. Suppose you were in danger of drowning. What would be an advantage of being in salt water?

   _____

   _____

   _____

4. What other factors might come into play as you consider whether you would rather be in fresh water or in salt water if you were in danger of drowning?

   _____

   _____

   _____

Activity   **Earth's Oceans**

Characteristics of Ocean Waves

Most waves are caused by wind. As a wave moves through water, the surface of the water rises and falls. The highest part of a wave is referred to as the crest; the lowest part is called the trough. The wave height is the difference in level between the crest and the trough. The wavelength is the distance between two successive crests or troughs.

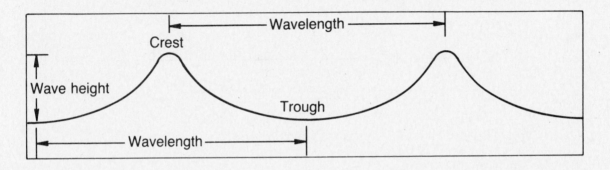

The time required for two successive crests or troughs to pass a certain point is referred to as the wave period. Wave speed can be calculated using the following relationship.

$$\text{wave speed} = \frac{\text{wavelength}}{\text{wave period}}$$

When waves move into shallow water, the troughs begin to drag along the bottom and slow down, while the crests continue at their normal speed. As a result, the front of the wave becomes steeper than the back of the wave. Eventually the crest topples over and the wave is said to break. Waves break in water that has a depth equal to approximately one-half the wavelength or about 1.3 times the wave height.

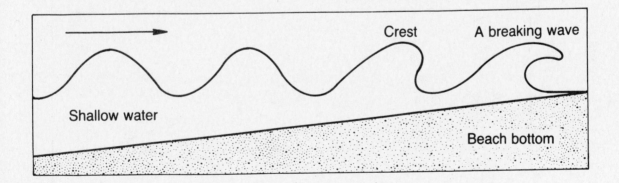

Use this information and the following diagram to answer questions 1 through 4.

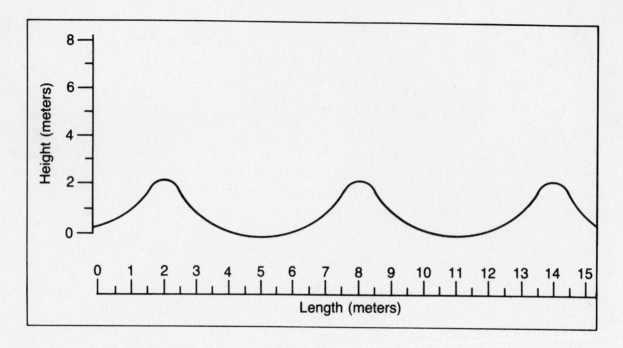

1. Label the wave crests and wave troughs on the diagram.

2. What is the wavelength? _____

3. What is the wave height? _____

4. What is the speed of the waves if the wave period is 4 seconds? _____

_____

Use the background information and the following diagram to answer questions 5 through 8.

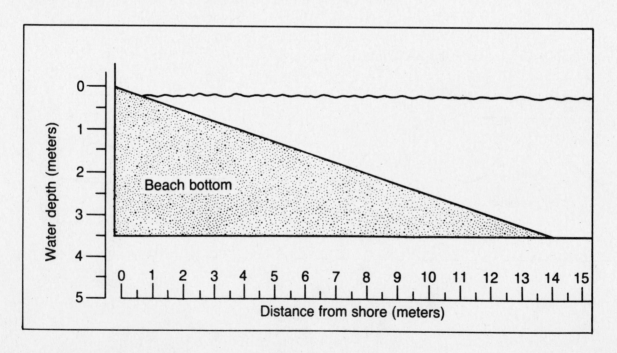

5. In what depth of water would a wave begin to break if it had a wavelength of 3 meters?

_____

_____

6. According to the diagram, how far from shore would a wave break that had a

wavelength of 3 meters? _____

7. What would the wave height be for the wave described in the previous two questions?

_____

_____

8. If increased winds caused an increase in wave heights, what would happen to the

distance from shore that the waves were breaking? _____

_____

Activity

Ocean and Continental Profiles

The ocean floor can be mapped with precision by using depth recorders aboard oceanographic survey ships. These recorders reflect sound waves off the ocean floor and receive the returning echoes as the ship moves across the ocean's surface. By determining the time it takes for the echoes to return, scientists can determine the depth of the ocean floor. In this activity you will look at profiles of the Atlantic and Pacific Ocean floors as well as a profile of the land surface across the United States. After looking at these profiles you will answer questions about each one.

Profiles are cross-sectional views of underwater or land surface features. These profiles are made by plotting ocean depth and land elevation in meters versus horizontal distance in kilometers. The vertical scale is different from the horizontal scale on these profiles. The difference in scales causes the vertical steepness of mountains to be exaggerated so that you can see them on these drawings.

The following profile shows the floor of the Atlantic Ocean from South America to Africa. Answer the following questions after you look at this profile. Zero on the vertical scale is represented by sea level on each of the profiles.

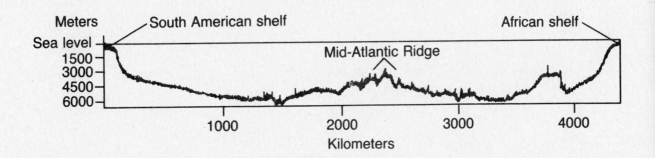

1. What is the greatest depth shown on this profile? _____

2. How far below the ocean's surface is the tallest peak in the Mid-Atlantic Ridge?

_____

3. Does this profile show a rift valley cutting through the Mid-Atlantic Ridge? _____

_____

4. Is the Mid-Atlantic Ridge the same height on both sides of the valley? _____

_____

The next profile shows the floor of the Pacific Ocean from the Island of Hawaii to Los Angeles, California. Answer the following questions after you look at this profile.

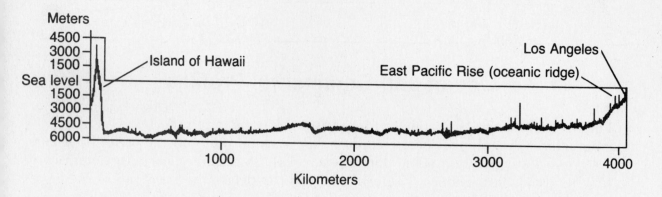

1. What is the greatest depth shown in this profile? _____

2. Is the continental shelf at Los Angeles as flat as the South American and African shelves shown in the previous profile? _____

3. Give a reason for the edge of the continent at Los Angeles being so irregularly shaped. _____

4. Are seamounts shown in this profile? _____

5. What is the height of the tallest peak in the profile as measured from the ocean floor? _____

The last profile shows the land surface across the United States. Answer the following questions after you look at this profile.

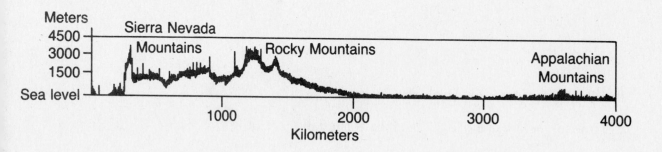

1. What is the height of the tallest peak in this profile? _____

2. Which mountains shown on this profile are the lowest in the United States? _____

_____

3. From sea floor to summit, are the Rocky Mountains higher than the Island of Hawaii? _____

Activity

The Salty Ocean

Salt is left behind during the ocean's hydrologic cycle. To demonstrate this process, use the following steps.

1. Obtain a hot plate, 1 L of water, a saucepan, and 5 g of salt.

2. Thoroughly mix 5 g of salt in 1 L of water.

3. Pour the solution into a saucepan.

4. Place the pan on a heat source. **CAUTION:** *Use extreme care when working with a hot plate.* In this activity the heat source represents the sun.

Soon the water will begin to boil and turn to vapor. In a few minutes all of the water will have turned to water vapor. You should notice a residue left behind on the bottom of the saucepan. This residue is the salt you mixed in the water.

5. Scrape out the residue and use a pan balance to find the mass of the salt.

How many grams of residue did you find? _____

Explain how fresh water can be obtained from salty ocean water. _____

_____

_____

_____

_____

In the space provided, draw a diagram of your experimental setup both before and after the heating.

Before Heating

After Heating

Activity   Earth's Oceans   CHAPTER **2**

Physical Properties of the Ocean's Life Zones

The oceans cover approximately 70 percent of the Earth's surface. Their depths can vary from 0 meters in the intertidal zone during low tide, to over 10,000 meters in the Pacific Ocean trenches. Life forms in the ocean range in size from microscopic diatoms to huge seaweeds over 90 meters long and whales that exceed 20 meters. The environments within the ocean vary greatly. Conditions near the ocean's surface are similar to those experienced at the Earth's surface in terms of temperature, pressure, and sunlight. Conditions found at great ocean depths include total darkness, water pressures that can crush submarines, and near freezing temperatures.

Since the conditions within the oceans vary so widely, scientists have divided the oceans into life zones based on certain physical properties and types of life forms that are present. The table below contains information about characteristics of ocean life zones. Use this information to identify the various life zones in the diagram on the next page. Write the name of each zone in the appropriate space on the diagram. Then answer the questions that follow.

Life Zones	Characteristic Properties
Intertidal Zone	• Located between the average high- and low-tide levels of the ocean over the continental shelf • Is alternately dry and wet as the tides change from low to high • Sunlight penetrates the entire zone.
Neritic Zone	• Located over the continental shelf between the average low-tide level of the ocean and the edge of the continental shelf • Is approximately 200 m thick at its maximum thickness • Sunlight penetrates the entire zone.
Open Sea Zone	• Includes all of the ocean beyond the continental shelf from the surface to the ocean basin floor
The open sea zone is divided into the following subdivisions:	
Photosynthetic Zone	• Extends from the ocean surface to approximately 200 m • Sunlight penetrates the entire zone.
Bathyal Zone	• Extends from approximately 200 m to 4000 m • Plants do not grow in the lower levels of this zone due to insufficient sunlight.
Abyssal Zone	• Extends from approximately 4000 m to about 6000 m • Always completely dark and water pressures may exceed 600 kg/cm^2

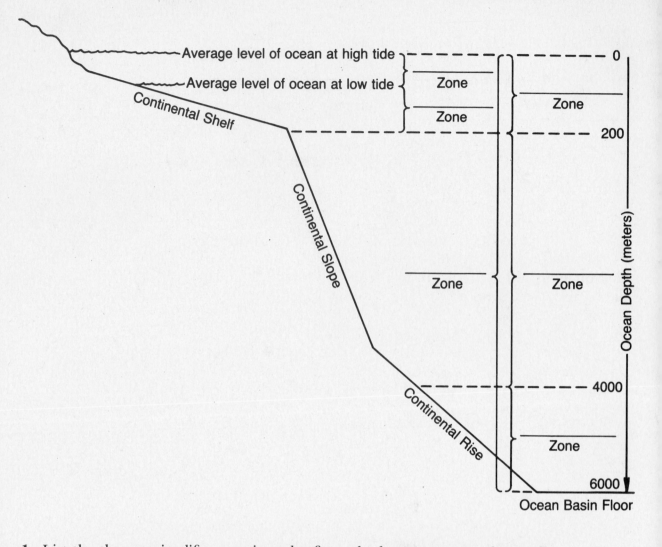

1. List the three major life zones in order from the largest zone to the smallest.

   a. _____

   b. _____

   c. _____

2. List the three divisions of the open sea zone in order from the division that is nearest to the ocean surface to the division that is farthest from the ocean surface.

   a. _____

   b. _____

   c. _____

3. Which subdivision of the open sea zone is most similar to the neritic zone?

   _____

4. The neritic zone and the photosynthetic zone both include the part of the ocean where sunlight penetrates easily to about 200 meters. Write at least two ways in which these zones differ.

_____

_____

_____

_____

5. a. Which life zones are easily penetrated by sunlight?

_____

_____

   b. Which life zones do not receive sufficient sunlight for plants to grow?

_____

_____

6. In which zone must plants and animals adapt to being exposed to the atmosphere for

   periods of time? _____

7. Which of the three major life zones contains the largest volume of ocean water?

_____

Determining Ocean Depth

1. The speed of sound in water is about 1500 m/sec. Sound waves given off by sonar instruments on board a ship take 8 seconds to travel to the ocean floor and back. How deep is the ocean floor?

Answer _____

2. Suppose it took sound waves 4 seconds to travel to the ocean floor and back. How deep would the ocean floor be?

Answer _____

3. If the depth of the ocean floor is 9000 meters, how long does it take sound waves to travel to the ocean floor?

Answer _____

ctivity

Temperature Effects and Surface Currents

Surface waters of the Earth's oceans are forced to move, primarily by winds. Where winds blow in the same direction for a long period of time, currents will develop that transport large masses of water over considerable distances across ocean surfaces. In this activity you will identify some surface currents and determine their effect on the temperatures of the continents they border. All you will need for this activity is a pencil or pen and colored pencils or crayons.

The following chart lists some surface currents in the ocean. Each current is identified with a number and classified as a cold or warm current. These same currents are represented by arrows and identified by numbers on the map on the next page.

Number	Name of Surface Current	Characteristic Temperature of Water Transported by Current
1	California Current	cold
2	Canary Current	cold
3	Gulf Stream	warm
4	Kuroshio Current	warm
5	East Australian Current	warm
6	Benguela Current	cold
7	Brazil Current	warm
8	Peru Current	cold
9	Antarctic Circumpolar Current	cold

1. Correctly identify each of the currents on the map on page 56 by labeling them in the spaces provided within the arrows.

2. Using two different colors, color the arrows that represent the cold-water currents in one color and the warm-water currents in another color. Include a key on the map to identify which colors represent the warm- and cold-water currents.

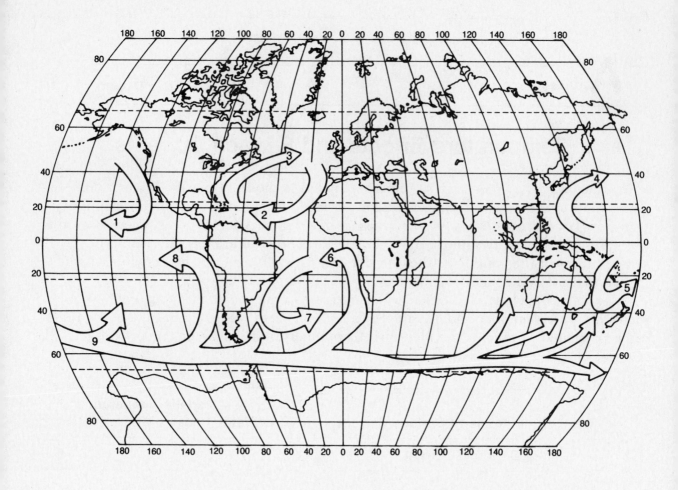

After identifying and coloring the currents on the map, answer the following questions.

1. The ocean currents on your map generally travel in either a clockwise or counterclockwise direction. Look at the ocean currents and compare the general direction followed by currents in the Northern Hemisphere with the direction of those in the Southern Hemisphere.

_____

_____

_____

2. Cold-water currents tend to have a cooling effect on the continental coastlines that they border, while warm-water currents tend to have a warming effect.

   a. Look at the pattern of currents in the Northern Hemisphere and describe the effect the currents have on the temperature of the coastal areas they border.

_____

_____

   b. Look at the pattern of currents in the Southern Hemisphere and describe the effect the currents have on the temperature of the coastal areas they border.

_____

_____

3. Look at the pattern of cold- and warm-water currents. What seems to determine

whether a current carries warm or cold water? _____

_____

_____

ctivity

Composition of Sea Water: Constructing a Graphic Model

Sea water, as the term suggests, is made up mostly of water. There are, however, other important ingredients dissolved in the water. In this activity you will construct a graphic model that illustrates the composition of sea water. All you will need to do this activity is a protractor and a pencil or pen.

Solid material that is dissolved in sea water is referred to as salts. Salts make up about 3.5 percent of the mass of sea water. The following chart lists the major dissolved salts that are present in sea water and identifies the number of grams of each salt contained in 100 grams of water.

**Salts Most Abundant
in Sea Water**

Dissolved Salts	Approximate Mass (in grams per 100 grams of sea water)
Sodium chloride, NaCl	2.72
Magnesium chloride, $MgCl_2$	0.38
Magnesium sulfate, $MgSO_4$	0.17
Calcium sulfate, $CaSO_4$	0.13
Potassium sulfate, K_2SO_4	0.08
Calcium carbonate, $CaCO_3$	0.01
Magnesium bromide, $MgBr_2$	0.008

1. Use the following equation and the information contained in the chart to calculate the percentage that each dissolved salt represents of the total mass of dissolved salts found in sea water. Enter your data in the appropriate space provided in the Data Table.

$$\text{Percentage of the total mass of dissolved salts} = \frac{\text{Mass of dissolved salts (grams)}}{3.5 \text{ grams}} \times 100$$

DATA TABLE

Dissolved Salts	Percentage of Total Mass of Dissolved Salts	Number of Degrees on Circle Graph
Sodium chloride, $NaCl$		
Magnesium chloride, $MgCl_2$		
Magnesium sulfate, $MgSO_4$		
Calcium sulfate, $CaSO_4$		
Potassium sulfate, K_2SO_4		
Calcium carbonate, $CaCO_3$		
Magnesium bromide, $MgBr_2$		

2. In the graphic model you will construct, 360° on the circle graph will equal 100 percent of the composition of dissolved salts in sea water. Therefore, 1 percent of dissolved salts will equal 3.6° on your graph. Convert each of the percentage values you calculated in the previous step to the appropriate number of degrees and enter your data in the spaces provided on the Data Table.

3. Using your protractor and the information from the Data Table, construct a graph in the circle that illustrates the composition of dissolved solids in sea water. Label each section of the graph.

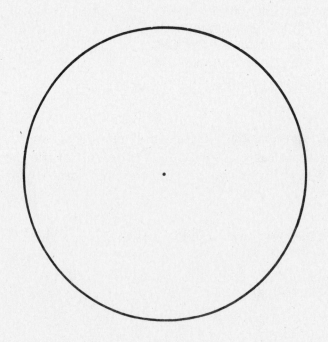

After you have completed your graph, answer the following questions.

1. a. Sea water is actually about 96.5 percent water. If you were going to construct a circle graph to illustrate the composition of sea water, how many degrees on the

   graph would be needed to represent water? _____

   b. On such a graph, how many degrees would be needed to represent the total of all

   of the dissolved salts contained in sea water? _____

2. If erosion continues to carry more and more dissolved salts into the oceans, after many thousands of years, how would you expect the composition of sea water to be

   different from how it is today? _____

   _____

   _____

3. Many animals that live in the ocean use some types of dissolved salts to build their shells. What would happen to the composition of sea water if these animals were to

   decrease drastically in number? _____

   _____

   _____

Activity _____ CHAPTER

Earth's Oceans **2**

Profile of a Tropical Ocean

Tropical ocean waters have certain physical characteristics, which include temperature and salinity. These two characteristics are influenced by variables that act on the ocean waters. The variables include amount of sunlight received, proximity to the equator, and seasonal effects associated with precipitation and with the discharge of major river systems thousands of kilometers upstream.

Ocean water is 96.5 percent pure water and 3.5 percent dissolved solids, such as salt, and dissolved gases, such as oxygen. The amounts of these dissolved substances remain relatively constant. The salinity of ocean water is measured in terms of parts (solid material) per thousand of ocean water.

Water can dissolve most substances, if only in very small amounts. Because some substances are very soluble in water, their concentration in the oceans is quite high. Approximately 95 percent of the dissolved solids in ocean water are six elements: chlorine, sodium, magnesium, sulfur, calcium, and potassium. The salts in ocean water come from the land and, to a lesser extent, from the evaporation of the ocean water.

Table 1   Salinity in Warm Tropical Waters

Depth (meters)	Parts per Thousand	
	Minimum	**Maximum**
0	34.40	35.98
50	34.77	36.20
100	36.20	37.00
150	36.52	37.20
200	36.50	37.10
250	36.40	36.97
300	36.20	36.80
350	35.93	36.60
400	35.67	36.35
450	35.43	36.09
500	35.23	35.78
550	35.07	35.53
600	34.92	35.33
650	34.88	35.22
700	34.83	35.10
750	34.80	35.03
800	34.80	34.97
850	34.83	34.93
900	34.87	34.93
950	34.90	34.97
1000	34.97	35.00

1. What is the minimum salinity level at the ocean surface? _____

   What is the maximum salinity level at the ocean surface? _____

2. What is the difference in salinity between the minimum and maximum levels at sea level? _____

3. What is the minimum salinity at a depth of 1000 meters? _____

   How does it differ from the maximum salinity at the same depth? _____

4. How does the minimum salinity level vary between sea level and a depth of 1000 meters? _____
   _____

   What might account for this difference? _____
   _____

The dissolved gases that warm ocean waters contain are mostly oxygen, carbon dioxide, and nitrogen. The concentration of these gases depends on their concentration in the atmosphere, their solubility, and the temperature and salinity of the ocean water.

Table 2 Dissolved Oxygen in Warm Tropical Waters

Depth (meters)	Milliliters per Liter	
	Minimum	Maximum
0	4.32	5.41
50	4.31	5.25
100	4.18	5.26
150	3.96	4.91
200	3.88	4.71
250	3.90	4.42
300	3.92	4.29
350	3.79	4.25
400	3.50	4.13
450	3.17	3.95
500	3.02	3.71
550	2.92	3.58
600	2.90	3.46
650	2.92	3.24
700	2.92	3.33
750	3.00	3.37
800	3.08	3.50
850	3.25	3.63
900	3.37	3.83
950	3.58	4.28
1000	3.78	4.30

The most abundant gas dissolved in ocean water is nitrogen. It is of little importance to the plant and animal life in the oceans, however. Oxygen enters ocean water through the process of photosynthesis, which is carried out by green plants in the ocean. Oxygen also enters the water from the atmosphere and from the rivers emptying into the ocean.

5. In what units is the amount of oxygen in ocean water measured? _____

_____

6. At which level in the ocean is the amount of dissolved oxygen the greatest? _____

_____

7. Scan the columns that show the amount of dissolved oxygen in ocean water. What happens to the amount of dissolved oxygen between sea level and a depth of 1000

meters? _____

_____

8. What might account for this variation in the amount of dissolved oxygen in ocean

water? _____

_____

_____

Solar energy and the properties of water itself determine the temperature of ocean water. Some scientists estimate that absorption of light energy accounts for more than 99 percent of the heat entering the sea. Only a small amount of the heat in the sea comes from the heat in the Earth's interior.

The amount of heat entering the sea is frequently equal to the amount of heat leaving the sea through the process of evaporation. Winds blowing over the ocean waters also cause the waters to cool off and evaporate.

The range of temperatures in the ocean is one of the factors that causes ocean currents and influences the location of marine organisms. The temperature of ocean water, like the salinity, remains fairly constant. This consistency in temperature maintains a balance in marine life and exerts a steady influence along the shoreline of neighboring land areas.

9. What factors influence the temperature of ocean water? _____

_____

_____

_____

10. How does the temperature of the tropical ocean water influence an area? _____

_____

_____

Table 3 Temperature in Warm Tropical Waters

Depth (meters)	Temperature (°C)											
	Jan.	Feb.	Mar.	Apr.	May	Jun.	Jul.	Aug.	Sept.	Oct.	Nov.	Dec.
0	26.5	26.2	26.2	26.5	27.5	27.9	28.2	28.4	28.8	29.2	28.6	27.6
10	26.5	26.2	26.2	26.5	27.5	27.9	28.2	28.3	28.8	29.0	28.6	27.5
20	26.5	26.2	26.2	26.3	27.5	27.9	28.1	28.3	28.6	29.0	28.6	27.5
30	26.4	26.2	26.1	26.3	27.3	27.8	28.1	28.2	28.6	28.8	28.7	27.7
40	26.3	26.2	25.9	26.5	27.3	27.8	28.1	28.0	28.4	28.8	28.8	27.9
50	26.2	26.2	25.8	26.5	26.7	27.5	27.9	27.9	27.5	28.7	28.4	27.6
60	26.0	26.2	25.7	26.4	26.3	27.2	27.4	27.6	27.0	27.9	27.6	27.4
70	26.1	26.2	25.7	25.8	25.8	26.6	26.9	26.8	26.6	27.0	26.9	27.0
80	25.9	26.0	25.4	25.8	25.3	25.9	26.2	26.0	26.2	26.3	26.3	26.0
90	25.6	25.6	25.5	25.3	25.0	25.4	25.8	25.6	25.5	25.5	25.6	25.5
100	25.3	25.5	25.1	25.0	24.6	25.0	25.2	25.0	25.1	25.5	24.7	24.9
150	22.3	22.9	22.8	22.8	22.0	22.0	22.6	22.0	22.8	22.9	22.5	22.0
200	19.9	20.0	20.1	19.8	19.5	19.7	20.2	20.1	20.0	20.3	19.7	19.5
250	18.0	18.1	18.3	17.9	18.2	17.9	18.1	18.0	18.2	18.4	17.8	17.5
300	16.9	17.0	16.9	16.6	16.5	16.8	16.8	16.9	17.0	17.0	16.9	16.4
350	16.0	15.7	15.6	15.6	14.9	15.5	15.5	15.5	15.8	15.8	15.4	15.1
400	14.3	14.1	14.2	14.4	13.7	14.1	14.2	14.2	14.3	14.1	14.0	14.1
450	13.5	12.9	12.9	13.2	12.3	12.6	13.0	12.9	13.0	13.1	13.0	12.8
500	12.6	11.6	11.8	11.2	11.5	10.8	11.8	11.9	12.0	12.3	11.2	11.8
600	10.0	10.0	9.5	9.4	9.5	9.5	9.5	9.6	9.8	9.8	9.5	10.0
700	7.9	8.0	7.7	7.7	7.7	8.0	7.9	8.0	8.0	8.2	7.9	8.2
800	6.5	6.5	6.6	6.6	6.4	6.6	6.4	6.6	6.7	6.6	7.0	6.9
900	5.8	6.1	5.9	5.9	5.8	5.8	5.9	5.9	5.9	6.0	6.1	6.0
1000	5.2	5.3	5.3	5.3	5.3	5.3	5.2	5.4	5.2	5.3	5.3	5.3
1100	4.8	4.9	4.9	4.9	4.9	4.8	4.9	4.9	4.9	4.8	4.8	4.8
1200	4.6	4.6	4.7	4.6	4.6	4.5	4.5	4.6	4.5	4.7	4.6	4.5
1300	4.4	4.4	4.4	4.4	4.4	4.4	4.4	4.4	4.4	4.5	4.5	4.4
1400	4.3	4.3	4.3	4.3	4.3	4.3	4.3	4.3	4.3	4.4	4.3	4.3
1500	4.2	4.2	4.2	4.2	4.2	4.2	4.2	4.2	4.2	4.3	4.2	4.2

11. What is the warmest water temperature at sea level? _____

12. During which month is the surface water of the ocean the warmest? _____

13. What is the greatest range in ocean temperature from the surface to a depth of 1500

meters? _____

14. During which month(s) is(are) the ocean temperature the coolest? _____

What would account for these temperatures? _____

15. What is the average temperature of ocean water at sea level for the year? _____

16. What major factor accounts for the fact that ocean temperature does not vary at a

depth of 1500 meters? _____

Major Features of the Earth's Solid Surface: Constructing a Graphic Model

The Earth's solid surface consists of a variety of features. Some are exposed above sea level, while others are found below sea level, and for the most part, hidden from direct observation. Because more than 70 percent of the Earth's surface is covered by water, most people have never seen and are unaware of most of the Earth's major features.

What are some of the major features? How impressive are they when compared with the total world surface? In this activity you will construct a graphic model that illustrates and compares how much of the Earth's solid surface each major feature occupies.

The following Data Table identifies the major features of the Earth's solid surface and lists their approximate surface areas as percentages of the total world surface. You will use this information to construct a circle graph. On this graphic model, 100 percent of the Earth's solid surface will equal 360° on the circle graph. Accordingly, each 1 percent of the total area that a given feature occupies will equal 3.6° on the circle graph.

DATA TABLE

	Type of Major Feature	Approximate Percentage of Total Solid Surface	Number of Degrees on Circle Graph
Features Below Sea Level	Ocean basin floor	30.0	
	Underwater volcanic mountains and hills	2.2	
	Ocean ridges	22.8	
	Continental shelf and slope	11.0	
	Continental rise	3.6	
Features Above Sea Level	Volcanic islands (mountains)	1.2	
	Continental mountains	10.3	
	Continental land masses	18.9	

First, convert each of the percentage values into the appropriate number of degrees and enter the data in the Data Table.

Then, using your protractor and the information you entered in the Data Table, construct a graph in the circle that shows what percentage of the Earth's solid surface each feature occupies. Correctly label each section of the circle graph with the name of each feature and the approximate percentage of total surface each occupies.

**Features Above
Sea Level**

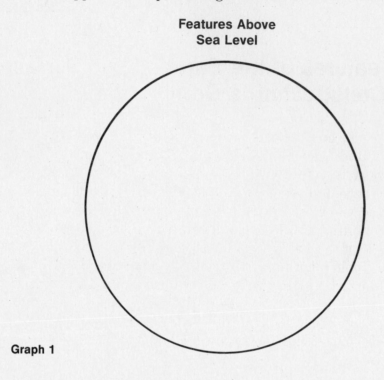

Graph 1

Now look at the next circle graph. The information provided in this graph shows the relative amount of the Earth's surface covered by oceans and continents. Using your protractor, determine the approximate percentages of the total land area and individual oceans on the Earth's surface. Remember that 3.6° of every section shown on the circle graph represents 1 percent of the Earth's total area.

Features Below Sea Level

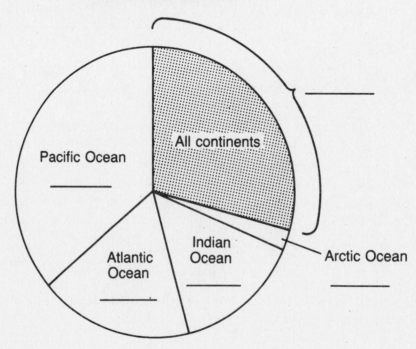

Graph 2

After you have completed both circle graphs, answer the following questions.

1. What percent of the Earth's surface is above sea level? _____

2. What percent of the Earth's surface is below sea level? _____

3. Which type of major surface feature takes up most of the Earth's total solid surface?

_____

Of the total, what percent does it represent? _____

4. a. What percent of the Earth's surface that is below sea level consists of ocean floor?

_____

b. What percent of the Earth's surface that is below sea level consists of oceanic

ridges? _____

5. a. What percent of the Earth's total surface consists of mountains of any type that

are above sea level? _____

b. What percent of the Earth's total surface consists of mountains of any type that

are below sea level? _____

c. What percent of the Earth's total surface consists of nonmountainous areas that

are above or below sea level? _____

6. a. If the level of the oceans fell during a future ice age so that all continental shelves
and slopes were exposed, by how much would the total land area above sea level

increase? _____

b. What percent of the Earth's total solid surface would exist below sea level under

such conditions? _____

7. Which of the following sets of percentages most nearly represents the distribution of
major features on the Earth's solid surface? Circle the letter of the correct answer.

a. Features above sea level: one-half
Features below sea level: one-half

b. Nonmountainous features: one-third
Mountainous features: two-thirds

c. Mountains and ridges: one-third
Continents and associated features: one-third
Ocean basins and miscellaneous features: one-third

8. What oceans and their percentages must be combined to equal the size of the Pacific

Ocean? _____

Exploring Planet Earth I ■ 71

_____ *Laboratory Investigation* _____

The Effect of Water Depth on Sediments

Problem
To determine the effects that differences in water depth have on the settling of sediments.

Materials *(per group)*
plastic tubes of different lengths that contain sediment samples and salt water

Procedure
1. Obtain a plastic tube from your teacher.
2. Make sure that both ends of the tube are securely capped.

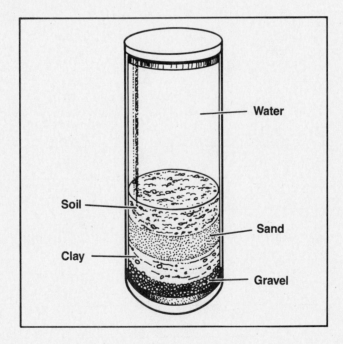

3. Hold the tube by both ends and gently tip it back and forth until the sediments in the tube are thoroughly mixed throughout the water.
4. Set the tube in an upright position in a place where it will not be disturbed.
5. Repeat steps 1 through 4 for each of the remaining tubes.
6. Carefully observe the sediments in each tube.

Observations

1. Make a detailed sketch to illustrate the heights of the different layers formed when the sediments in each tube settled.

2. What general statement can you make about the size of the sediment particles and the order in which each type of sediment settled in the tube? _____

_____

_____

Analysis and Conclusions

1. What effect does the length of the water column have on the number and types of sediment layers formed in each tube? _____

_____

_____

2. How are these tubes accurate models of what happens to sediments carried to the ocean? _____

_____

_____

3. What is the variable present in this investigation? What variables that may be present in the ocean are not tested in this investigation? _____

_____

_____

4. **On Your Own**   Design an investigation to determine the effect of different amounts of salinity on the formation of sediment layers.

Answer Key

Chapter Discovery: Help! I'm Drowning

Procedure 5. 8 **10.** 11 **11.** Answers will vary. **Critical Thinking and Application 1.** Each time salt was added, the straw should float higher in the water. **2.** Objects float more easily in salt water. **3.** It would be easier to float in salt water. You might be able to keep yourself above the surface of salt water by expending less energy. **4.** Accept all reasonable answers. Factors such as currents, water temperature, depth of water, the danger of swallowing salt water, and the presence of dangerous ocean animals are factors that may influence survival in salt water.

Activity: Characteristics of Ocean Waves

1. Crests are the highest points of waves; troughs are the lowest points. **2.** 6 m
3. 2 m **4.** 6 m ÷ 4 sec = 1.5 m/sec **5.** It would break in water at a depth equal to approximately one-half a wavelength, or in about 1.5 m of water. **6.** It would break about 5.8 m from shore. **7.** 0.5 × wavelength = 1.3 × wave height. By substitution, 0.5 × 3 m = 1.3 × wave height; 1.5 m = 1.3 × wave height. Therefore, wave height = 1.5 m ÷ 1.3 = 1.15 m. **8.** As the wave height increased, the distance from the shore that the waves were breaking would increase.

Activity: Ocean and Continent Profiles

Vertical exaggeration is about 100 × on all profiles. **First Profile 1.** about 6000 meters **2.** about 2000 meters **3.** Yes.
4. No. **Second Profile 1.** about 6000 meters **2.** No. **3.** The East Pacific Rise, an oceanic ridge, extends up the California coast. **4.** Yes. **5.** about 9500 meters
Third Profile 1. about 4000 meters
2. Appalachian Mountains **3.** No.

Discovery Activity: The Salty Ocean

About two-thirds of the total mineral content of the oceans is sodium chloride, or ordinary salt. The concentration of salt varies in different parts of the ocean. For example, because salt dissolves more rapidly in warmer water, salt is found in larger concentrations in tropical waters than in polar waters. Near the mouths of large rivers, where great amounts of fresh water enter the ocean daily, the percentage of salt is smaller.

Activity: Physical Properties of the Ocean's Life Zones

Diagram top to bottom, left to right: Intertidal   Neritic   Open Sea   Photosynthetic   Bathyal   Abyssal
Questions 1. a. Open Sea   b. Neritic   c. Intertidal **2.** a. Photosynthetic   b. Bathyal   c. Abyssal **3.** Photosynthetic (sunlight penetrates easily). **4.** Answers may include the following: the neritic zone doesn't extend upward to the ocean surface and the photosynthetic zone does; the neritic zone is over the continental shelf and the photosynthetic zone is in the open ocean; most plants in the neritic zone are attached, while those in the photosynthetic zone are free-floating. **5.** a. the intertidal and neritic and the photosynthetic subdivision of the open sea zone   b. the bathyal and abyssal subdivisions of the open sea zone **6.** the intertidal **7.** the open sea zone

Problem-Solving Activity: Determining Ocean Depth

1. 8 sec ÷ 2 = 4 sec × 1500 m/sec = 6000 m. Students should realize that the distance sound waves travel to the ocean floor and back in 8 seconds is twice the depth of the ocean floor. **2.** 4 sec ÷ 2 = 2 sec × 1500 m/sec = 3000 m **3.** 9000 m ÷ 1500 m/sec = 6 sec

Activity: Temperature Effects and Surface Waves

Check maps to be sure students have filled them in correctly. **1.** Surface ocean currents in the Northern Hemisphere generally travel in a clockwise direction, while ocean currents in the Southern Hemisphere generally travel in a counterclockwise direction. **2.** a. Surface ocean currents in the Northern Hemisphere tend to warm eastern coastal areas and cool western coastal areas. b. Surface ocean currents in the Southern Hemisphere tend to warm eastern coastal areas and cool western coastal areas, just as in the Northern Hemisphere. **3.** Currents traveling toward the equator tend to carry cold water from the higher latitudes, while currents traveling away from the equator tend to carry warm water from the warm equatorial region.

Problem-Solving Activity: Composition of Sea Water: Constructing a Graphic Model

Data Table Sodium chloride: 77.71, 279.77; Magnesium chloride: 10.86, 39.09; Magnesium sulfate: 4.86, 17.49; Calcium sulfate: 3.71, 13.37; Potassium sulfate: 2.29, 8.23; Calcium carbonate: 0.29, 1.03; Magnesium bromide: 0.23, 0.82. To convert the percentage value to the appropriate number of degrees for the graph, merely multiply the percentage value by 3.6°. Check students' graphs for accuracy. **Questions 1.** a. $96.5 \times 3.6° = 347.4°$ b. $3.5 \times 3.6° = 12.6°$ **2.** Assuming that the present pattern continues, the composition of salts relative to each other should remain constant; however, the total percentage of sea water that is made up of dissolved salts will continue to increase. **3.** There would be an increase in the salts normally used by the shelled animals relative to the other salts and the total percentage of sea water that is made up of dissolved salts would increase above the 3.5% value.

Activity: Profile of a Tropical Ocean

1. 34.4 ppt, 35.98 ppt **2.** 1.58 ppt **3.** 34.97 ppt, .03 ppt **4.** It increases as the depth approaches 200 m, then decreases, and then increases as the depth reaches 1000 m. Answers might include proximity to coastline, proximity to major river systems, deep ocean currents. **5.** milliliters per liter **6.** surface **7.** It decreases as the depth approaches 650

m and then increases. **8.** Answers will vary but will probably include the idea that deep ocean currents with their extremely cold water cause a concentration of specific minerals, nutrients, and gases. **9.** solar energy and the properties of water **10.** Water temperature causes the summer to be somewhat cooler and the winter somewhat warmer. **11.** 29.2° **12.** October **13.** 24.9° **14.** February and March. Starting in December, ocean water receives the least amount of direct solar rays over an extended period of time. There is continued cooling of the water, which finally reaches its maximum cooling in February and March. **15.** 27.5° **16.** very little sunlight

Activity: Major Features of the Earth's Solid Surface: Making a Graphic Model

Data Table and Graph 1 108.0°, 7.9°, 82.1°, 39.6°, 12.0°, 4.3°, 37.1°, 68.0°. To convert the percentage values to the approximate number of degrees, multiply each percentage value by 3.6°. **Graph 2** All continents 29.2 percent, Arctic Ocean 2.4 percent, Indian Ocean 14.5 percent, Atlantic Ocean 18.4 percent, Pacific Ocean 35.4 percent **Questions 1.** 30.4 percent **2.** 60.6 percent **3.** ocean basin floor, 30 percent **4.** a. 43.1 percent b. 32.8 percent **5.** a. 11.5 percent b. 25.0 percent c. 63.5 percent **6.** a. 11 percent b. 58.6 percent **7.** c **8.** Atlantic 18.4 percent + Indian 14.6 percent + Arctic 2.4 percent = Pacific 35.4 percent

Laboratory Investigation: The Effect of Water Depth on Sediments

Observations 1. Sketches will vary, depending on the contents of each tube, but they should accurately display the arrangement of the contents of each tube. **2.** The largest particles will generally settle first and will be found at the bottom of the tube. **Analysis and Conclusions 1.** The greatest degree of sorting occurs in the longest tube. That is, the most clearly differentiated layers are formed in that tube. **2.** The ocean contains varying depths, similar to the varying depths of water in the tubes. **3.** The depth of the water; ocean currents, water temperature, water density, salinity, and so on. **4.** Investigations will vary. Check each design to ensure that it will determine the effect of different amounts of salinity on the formation of sediment layers.

Contents

*Appropriate for cooperative learning

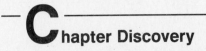

Chapter Discovery

Earth's Fresh Water

Hard Water/Soft Water

Background Information

The water that comes out of the tap in your home or school may be "hard" or "soft." Hard water contains large amounts of dissolved minerals, such as calcium and magnesium. Soft water does not contain these minerals.

Materials

piece of chalk (calcium carbonate)
borax or washing soda
plastic bag with tie
hammer
glass or plastic container that pours easily
3 large clear jars with lids
teaspoon
paper coffee filter
soap powder
masking tape
marking pen

Procedure

1. Label one jar "H" for hard and another jar "S" for soft.

2. Put the piece of chalk in the plastic bag and secure the tie. Use the hammer to break the chalk into small pieces. **CAUTION:** *Be careful when using the hammer.* Do not let the bag come open, as pieces of chalk could fly up and injure you.

3. Open the bag. Use the head of the hammer or a spoon to grind the pieces of chalk into a fine powder.

4. Fill the glass or plastic container about two-thirds full with water. Add the powdered chalk to the water and stir well.

5. Place the paper filter over the jar marked "H" and pour the chalk and water mixture through the filter into the jar. Keep pouring until the jar is half full.

6. Repeat step 5 with the jar marked "S."

7. To the jar marked "S," add two teaspoons of borax or washing soda and stir.

8. Add a teaspoon of soap powder to each jar. Place the lids on the jars and close tightly. Shake each jar until suds form. (If you don't get suds, add another teaspoon of soap powder to each jar.)

9. Fill the remaining jar about half full with tap water. Add a teaspoon of soap powder (make sure you add the same amount as you did to the jars marked H and S), close tightly, and shake.

Observations

1. What do you notice about the amount of suds produced in each jar? _____

_____

_____

_____

2. What do you notice about the amount of suds produced in this jar? How does it compare to the suds produced in step 8?

_____

_____

_____

Critical Thinking and Application

1. What can you conclude about the action of soap in hard water and in soft water? Why? _____

_____

_____

_____

2. Homeowners who have hard water often purchase water softeners. What types of substances would you expect a water softener to contain? _____

_____

_____

_____

3. Look at your results in step 9. Would you say that the water coming out of your tap is hard or soft? Why? _____

_____

_____

_____

Activity

The Water Cycle

Fill in the correct terms in the spaces labeled a through h using the following terms:

Condensation
Evaporation and transpiration
From the ocean
From plants and soil

Groundwater
Runoff
From lakes and streams
Precipitation

Studying the Water Cycle

Falling drops of rain, the formation of clouds, moving water in a stream, and evaporation are parts of a series of events that occur over and over in an endless cycle. There are many cycles in nature that affect our lives; however, these particular events are all parts of the water cycle.

Process	Description
Evaporation	Process by which liquid water changes to water vapor
Transpiration	Process by which water evaporates from the leaves of plants
Condensation	Process by which water vapor changes to liquid water
Runoff	Process by which water flows over the surface of the ground
Precipitation	Process by which water, in any form, falls from the atmosphere to the Earth's surface

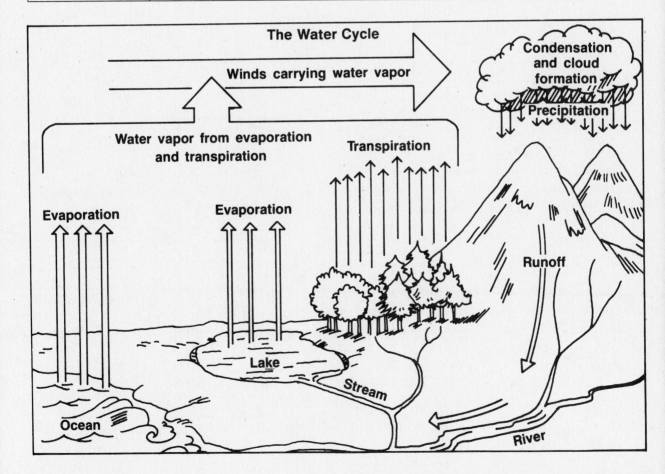

The Water Cycle

When precipitation, in the form of water, falls to the Earth's surface, three things can happen to it. It can run off, evaporate or transpire back into the atmosphere, or soak into the Earth's surface. Approximately 64 percent of the water that falls either evaporates or transpires and about 25 percent runs off. What percentage of the precipitation soaks in?

Correctly complete the following diagram by selecting the terms from the list of processes and placing them in the appropriate spaces.

Processes:

Runoff

Condensation

Precipitation

Cloud formation

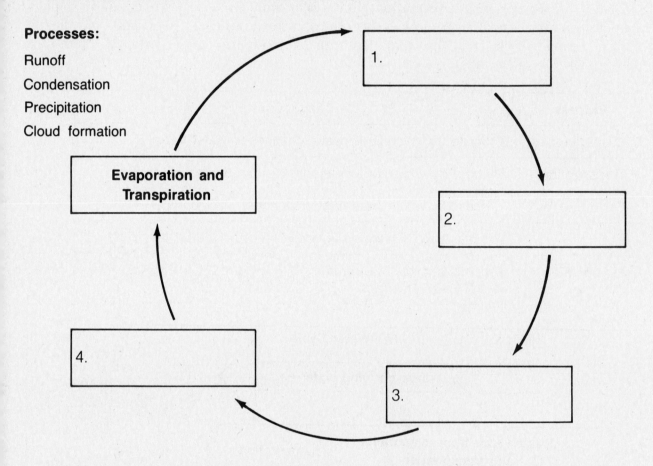

Evaporation and transpiration are the only two processes that return water to the atmosphere. Since oceans cover approximately 70 percent of the Earth's surface, explain why evaporation places more water vapor into the atmosphere than transpiration.

About 99 percent of the Earth's water supply is either in the salty oceans or frozen in the form of ice or snow. Only about 1 percent of the water on the Earth is in a form that people can use. Explain how the water cycle is important in providing a supply of fresh water.

On the water cycle diagram, draw two different possible paths that a water molecule might follow through the water cycle.

Stalactite and Stalagmite Formation

1. Fill two 500-mL graduated beakers with water.

2. Mix into each beaker enough salt to saturate the solution. (A saturated solution is one in which no more salt can be dissolved.)

3. Place the beakers approximately 10 cm apart on a stable tabletop or shelf. Between the two mixtures, place a 20-cm length of yarn or thick string. Let the ends hang down into the saturated water solutions.

4. During the next few days, observe the buildup of salt on both the table and the string or yarn.

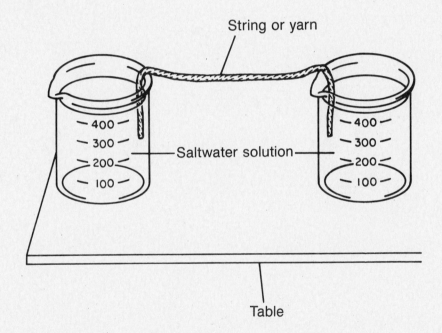

How is this experiment similar to stalactite and stalagmite formation in caverns?

_____

_____

_____

_____

_____

Activity

Icebergs

Using reference materials and current newspapers and magazines, find out more about icebergs. Draw a map of the world and indicate the areas where most icebergs can be found.

In a written report, explain how some scientists have proposed to use icebergs as a source of fresh water. Use the space below to outline your ideas.

_____

_____

_____

_____

_____

_____

_____

_____

_____

Activity

Water Budget

A budget is a record of income and outgo. In a water budget, precipitation such as rain or snow is the income. Evaporation is the outgo.

For this activity, you will need graph paper and two different colored pencils. On the graph paper, draw two axes. The vertical axis represents the precipitation. The horizontal axis represents the months.

Using the information in the chart and a colored pencil, plot a line graph of the monthly precipitation for city A. Using a different colored pencil, plot a line showing the evaporation on the same axes.

Now shade in the area where the precipitation is greater than the evaporation with one of the colored pencils. Label this area "Excess." Shade in the area where the evaporation is greater than the precipitation with the colored pencil. Label this area "Shortage."

Using the chart, find the excess or shortage for each month. To do this, subtract the evaporation from the precipitation. Record these results in the row labeled "Precipitation-Evaporation." A positive value indicates an excess, while a negative value is a shortage. Add the numbers across the "Precipitation" and "Evaporation" rows and enter the yearly totals. To find the yearly excess or shortage, subtract the total evaporation from the total precipitation.

	Monthly Precipitation and Evaporation (in mm) for City A												
	Jan.	Feb.	Mar.	Apr.	May	June	July	Aug.	Sept.	Oct.	Nov.	Dec.	Total
Precipitation	15	20	30	60	80	110	95	80	70	55	40	20	
Evaporation	0	0	15	40	95	130	155	120	75	45	5	0	
Precipitation–Evaporation													

1. Which month shows the greatest amount of precipitation? _____

2. Which month shows the greatest amount of evaporation? _____

3. a. Which months show an excess? _____

   b. A shortage? _____

4. a. How does an excess occur? _____

_____

   b. A shortage? _____

_____

5. How can you tell if there was an excess or a shortage at the end of the year?

_____

_____

_____

Activity

Water Pressure: A Hidden Community Worker

Water in and on the ground is frequently found under pressure. Air is always pressing and pushing on the water. The pull of gravity affects water pressure. Pressure can be placed on water by artificial means. Pumps are frequently used for this purpose. Because of water pressure, water can be made available for many important purposes that benefit our lives. These include the generation of electric power, the use of water in irrigation and sprinkler systems, water movement and use within our homes and businesses, fire extinguishers, and things as simple as a water fountain.

In this activity you will demonstrate water pressure principles and apply these principles to your environment.

You will need the following materials for this activity: several plastic bottles of different sizes and shapes with caps (soda pop bottles, milk bottles, and bleach bottles work well), small nail, tape, and water. Remember to observe all necessary safety precautions.

Procedure

1. Select several plastic bottles.

2. Using the small nail, punch three small holes up the side of each bottle. The holes should be at the same level on each bottle.

3. Place a small piece of tape over each hole.

4. Fill each bottle with water to the same level above the top hole. Do not put the caps on the bottles.

5. One bottle at a time, quickly remove the tape and observe what happens. Record your observations.

6. Repeat the procedure with the caps on the bottles. Record your observations.

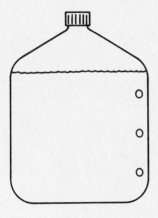 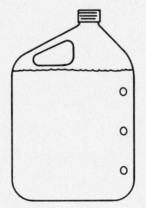 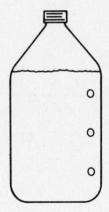

Observations

Bottles without caps

_____

_____

_____

Bottles with caps

_____

_____

_____

Critical Thinking and Application

1. Which stream of water coming from the side of each bottle had the greatest pressure?

   _____

   Why? _____

   _____

2. Does the water in the bottles with the caps on or the water in the bottles with the caps off have the greatest pressure?

   _____

3. What is the source of the pressure exerted on the water? _____

   _____

4. Does the total water pressure affect the rate at which the water flows from the holes?

   _____

5. What do you predict would happen to the escaping water if

   a. the holes were larger? _____

   _____

   b. the holes were smaller? _____

   _____

   c. you conducted the experiment at the top of Mount Everest? _____

   _____

    d. you plugged the bottom hole? _____

_____

    e. you attached an air pump to the bottle and increased the pressure? _____

_____

6. Does your community have a water tower or storage tank? _____

What is its purpose? _____

_____

7. If your community does not have a water tower or storage tank, what is the source of water pressure for your community?

_____

8. List the ways in which water under pressure is used in and around

    a. your school. _____

    _____

    b. your home. _____

    _____

    c. your community. _____

    _____

9. How might these water pressure principles apply to the construction of a dam that would use falling water to produce electricity? _____

_____

_____

_____

10. The hole in the side of the bottle is called an orifice. What would happen if the orifice were larger? _____

If the orifice were smaller? _____

11. Look up the word *penstock*. Give its definition and use it correctly in a sentence of your own composition. _____

_____

_____

12. How might a valve be used to affect or control water pressure? _____

_____

_____

Activity

Distillation and Desalination: Fresh Water From Salt Water

An adequate supply of fresh, clean water is essential to most living things. However, fresh water is in limited supply and could become even more limited in the future. Fresh water is not distributed evenly throughout the Earth. Some regions have more fresh water than others. In some places, the fresh water is full of minerals, chemicals, and salts. It is generally referred to as hard water. Groundwater frequently contains salts and minerals, especially in areas near mountains and in desert regions. Of course, the ocean is salt water too.

A process that can remove salts and minerals from water is called distillation. When distillation is used to remove salt from water, the process is called desalination. If desalination could be economically achieved on a large scale, it would mean an abundance of fresh water for areas of the world that lack an adequate water supply.

In this activity you will use a simple experiment to demonstrate the principle of distillation. You will then relate the principle to solving a contemporary water-supply problem.

You will need the following materials for this activity:

Bunsen burner   salt
ring stand with support ring   shallow pan
wire grid   ice
weight   flexible straw
water glass   flask
rubber stopper with one hole in it   piece of cardboard

Remember to observe all safety rules when working with a Bunsen burner and glassware.

Procedure

1. Pour a glass of water into the flask.
2. Add one tablespoon of salt to the water in the flask and stir until dissolved. Taste one drop of this solution.
3. Place the flask over the Bunsen burner by setting up the apparatus as shown in the accompanying diagram.
4. Insert the straw into the hole of the rubber stopper. Seal around the straw with clay if necessary to obtain a good seal.
5. Put the stopper in the flask. Make sure the straw is above the surface of the solution.
6. Bend the straw so that it can be inserted through a hole in the piece of cardboard.

7. Place the cardboard over the water glass and keep it in place with the weight if necessary.

8. Put the ice in the shallow pan and place the glass in it. Surround the glass with the ice.

9. Bring the solution to a boil.

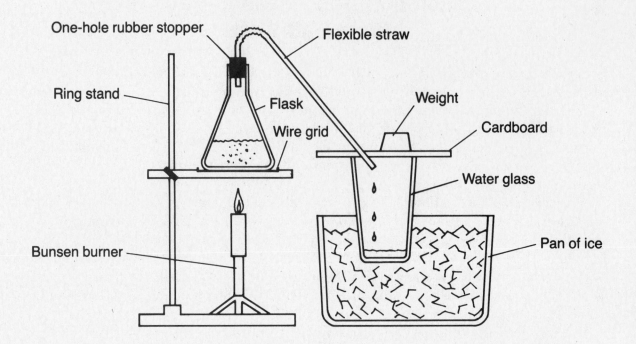

10. Observe what happens. Continue heating the solution until a distillate has accumulated in the glass. Turn off the Bunsen burner and allow the flask and distillate to cool. When the distillate has cooled, taste a drop of it.

11. Record your observations.

_____

_____

_____

_____

_____

12. When the apparatus has cooled completely, dismantle it and clean it according to appropriate laboratory procedures.

Critical Thinking and Application

1. What is the distillate in the bottom of the glass?

_____

2. How does it differ from the salt solution? _____

_____

3. Once the water in the flask was boiled off, what remained?

_____

4. What function did the ice in the pan serve? _____

_____

5. Does the distillation process occur in nature? _____

   If so, what remains in the landscape? _____

_____

6. In what geographic regions would you expect most natural distillation to occur?

_____

7. How does this process relate to the hydrologic cycle? _____

_____

8. How could distillation or desalination help a community whose future supply of fresh

   water is limited? _____

_____

Going Further

1. Try to determine if there are any distillation or desalination plants in your state. If so, write a report about them and report your findings to the class.

2. Find out about the procedure used to construct a survival still, which can provide water in the desert. Construct one. Demonstrate how the still works to the class.

Wise Use of Fresh Water

How much water do you use in a day? How about your family? Will your water supply last indefinitely?

Each person influences the quantity of fresh water removed from the ground. In addition to their daily needs, many of the activities of people and industries place demands on the quantity of fresh water withdrawn from the ground. It is important to note that only a small amount of this water ever returns to the groundwater system.

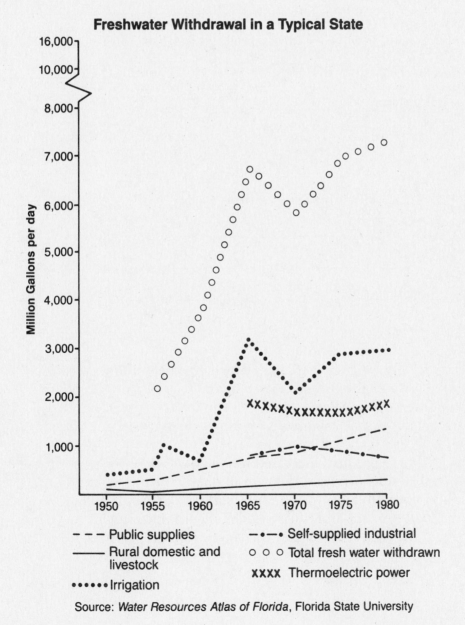

Freshwater Withdrawal in a Typical State

Legend:
- – – Public supplies
- —— Rural domestic and livestock
- •••• Irrigation
- —•—• Self-supplied industrial
- o o o Total fresh water withdrawn
- xxxx Thermoelectric power

Source: *Water Resources Atlas of Florida*, Florida State University

1. Describe the trend in the removal of fresh water over the past 30 years. _____

_____

_____

2. What factors do you think are responsible for this trend? _____

_____

_____

_____

3. Which activity of people makes the greatest demand on the freshwater supply?

_____

4. What was the maximum consumption of fresh water in millions of gallons per day?

_____

5. Use your monthly water bill to find out how much fresh water your family uses in a

particular month. How does this compare with other months? _____

_____

How does this compare with the families of other members of your class? _____

_____

What might account for any observed differences? _____

_____

_____

_____

_____

   As the demand for fresh water increases, people are beginning to realize that good-quality drinking water is essential. Water quality is based on the physical, chemical, and biological condition of the water. The environmental department in your state determines water quality by analyzing water samples for temperature, clarity, amount of dissolved oxygen, and amount of nutrient material.

   Increased use of water requires increased monitoring and evaluation of its quality. As the demand for fresh water increases, the overall quality of the water often decreases as a result of the addition of pollutants to the water supply. Agents of pollution can also harm other parts of the environment and cause possible health hazards. In turn, these pollutants can affect the water supply and the ways in which people can use the water.

Common Pollutants

Category	Examples	Possible Health and Environmental Effects	Affected Water Uses	Principal Sources
Oxygen-demanding materials	Sewage, paper manufacturing wastes	Deficiencies in oxygen levels that can stunt growth and reproduction of aquatic species; can also cause fish mortality	Water supply, recreation, fishing and fish propagation	Domestic waste, industrial waste, urban and agricultural runoff
Infectious agents (bacteria and viruses)	*E. coli* (indicator species), *Salmonella typhosa*	Diseases in humans and animals; can cause fish mortality	Water supply, recreation	Domestic waste, agricultural runoff
Nutrients	Nitrogen, phosphorus	High levels can cause excessive aquatic plant and algae growth and can contribute to fish mortality	Water supply, recreation, fishing and fish propagation, boating	Domestic and industrial waste, many land-use activities
Toxic substances	Ammonia, mercury, lead	Cancer, injury, or death in living organisms, including humans and all aquatic species	Water supply, recreation, fisheries, agriculture	Industrial waste, agricultural runoff (pesticides, herbicides)
Thermal pollutants	Power plant discharges	Fish and manatee mortality; shifts in structure of biological community	Fisheries	Power plants, industrial processing
Sediments and minerals	Sand, silt, clay	Cover substrate and increased aquatic species mortality	Water supply, recreation, fisheries, navigation	Many land-use activities
Oil and hazardous substances	Oil, gasoline, PCBs	Fish, bird, and other animal mortality	All uses	Industrial waste, urban stormwater, highway runoff

Exploring Planet Earth I ■ 101

6. Why is good-quality drinking water essential? _____

_____

7. How is the quality of drinking water determined? _____

_____

_____

8. How many categories of common pollutants affect water quality? _____

_____

9. Oxygen-demanding materials cause a decrease in the oxygen level of water and are harmful to fish and other aquatic animals. What are the principal sources of pollution that cause this to happen? _____

_____

_____

10. What are the most common water uses that pollutants affect? _____

_____

_____

11. What kind of pollution is caused by power plants? _____

12. What toxic substances may cause cancer, injury, or death to humans? ____

_____

13. People who are involved in agricultural activities depend on pesticides and herbicides. How are these substances helpful? _____

_____

_____

Harmful? _____

_____

_____

Laboratory Investigation

Porosity of Various Soils

Problem
How can the water-holding capability, or porosity, of various soils be determined?

Materials *(per group)*
250 mL sand   4 small paper cups
250 mL clay   2 L water
250 mL gravel   500-mL graduated cylinder

Procedure 🔺
1. Fill the first paper cup about three-fourths full of sand. Fill the second paper cup about three-fourths full of clay. Fill the third paper cup about three-fourths full of gravel. Fill the fourth paper cup about three-fourths full of a mixture of sand, clay, and gravel.

2. Fill the graduated cylinder with water to the 500 mL mark. Slowly pour water into the first cup. Let the water seep through the sand. Slowly add more water until a small pool of water is visible on the surface of the sand. At this point, the sand can hold no more water.

3. Determine the amount of water you added to the sand by subtracting the amount of water left in the graduated cylinder from 500 mL. Record this figure in the appropriate place in a data table similar to the one shown here.

4. Repeat steps 2 and 3 for the cups of clay, gravel, and the mixture of sand, clay, and gravel.

Observations

1. Which soil sample holds the most water? _____

2. Which soil sample holds the least water? _____

Soil	Amount of Water Added to Soil
Sand	
Clay	
Gravel	
Sand, clay, gravel	

Analysis and Conclusions

1. Why can some soil samples hold more water than others? _____
_____
_____

2. What can you conclude about the porosity of the soil samples you used?
_____
_____

3. If you wished to test the porosity of the soil found on your school grounds, what procedure would you follow? Which tested soil sample do you think the soil of the grounds at your school would most resemble? _____
_____
_____

4. **On Your Own** What effects, if any, do the roots of plants have on the porosity of soil? Design an experiment to test your hypothesis.

Answer Key

Chapter Discovery: Hard Water/Soft Water

Observations **1.** Soft water should produce more suds than hard water. **2.** Amount of suds should be similar to the amount produced in the jar marked "H" if the water is hard, or the amount produced in the jar marked "S" if the water is soft. **Critical Thinking and Application** **1.** Soap seems to work much better, or at least produce more suds, in soft water. This conclusion is based on the observation that the soap powder added to the jar marked "S" produced more suds. **2.** Something that is chemically similar to borax or washing soda, which was used in this activity. **3.** Answers will depend on whether the amount of suds produced more closely resembled the suds produced in the jar that contained hard water or the jar that contained soft water.

Activity: The Water Cycle

a. Precipitation   b. Runoff   c. Groundwater
d. From the ocean   e. From plants and soil
f. From lakes and streams   g. Evaporation and transpiration   h. Condensation

Problem-Solving Activity: Studying the Water Cycle

Text question If approximately 64 percent of the water that falls either evaporates or transpirates and 25 percent runs off, 11 percent of the precipitation soaks in: 100 − (64 + 25) = 11. **Diagram** **1.** condensation **2.** cloud formation **3.** precipitation **4.** runoff **Text question** Transpiration takes place from plants that live on only about 30 percent of the Earth's surface. Since evaporation takes place from about 70 percent of the Earth's surface, evaporation logically puts much more water into the atmosphere. **Text question** Since people must depend on such a small percentage of the total water supply, it is essential that water be recycled rapidly for reuse. **Text question**

A water molecule might follow one path—condensation, runoff, evaporation (ocean)—or another path—condensation, transpiration.

Problem-Solving Activity: Stalactite and Stalagmite Formation

Students should observe that salt buildup occurs on the yarn or string and also on the table from drippings from the yarn or string. Over time, the drippings should resemble the formation of stalactites and stalagmites.

Activity: Icebergs

Maps should show most icebergs along the Rose Ice Shelf in the Antarctic, near the Antarctic continent, and along the coast of Greenland in the northern Atlantic Ocean. Reports should mention that scientists have suggested towing icebergs to arid lands.

Problem-Solving Activity: Water Budget

Chart Jan. + 15; Feb. + 20; Mar. + 30; Apr. + 35; May − 15; June − 20; July − 60; Aug. − 40; Sept. − 5; Oct. + 10; Nov. + 35; Dec. + 25. Total precipitation: 695; total evaporation: 665. **Questions** **1.** June **2.** June **3.** a. Jan., Feb., Mar., Apr., Oct., Nov., Dec.   b. May, June, July, Aug., Sept. **4.** a. An excess occurs if the precipitation is greater than the evaporation.   b. A shortage occurs if the precipitation is less than the evaporation. **5.** Subtract the total evaporation from the total precipitation.

Discovery Activity: Water Pressure: A Hidden Community Worker

Critical Thinking and Application **1.** The stream coming out of the bottom hole had the greatest pressure because there is greater water pressure at that level. **2.** The bottles with caps off have the greatest pressure. **3.** The air pressure and the weight of the water. **4.** Yes. **5.** a. Water comes out more quickly, the pressure drops quickly. b. Water comes out more slowly, the pressure lasts longer. c. Water pressure is lower. d. Water flow increases slightly in the upper holes. e. Water would flow more quickly and squirt farther. **6.** The purpose of a water tower or storage tank is to store water and provide water pressure. **7.** Answers will vary. **8.** Answers will vary but may include the following: school—drinking fountains, rest rooms, showers, lawn watering, fire extinguisher, kitchen; home—showers, sinks, dishwasher, lawn watering, radiators; community—parks, fountains, swimming pools **9.** The water needs to flow under pressure through the dam. The greater the flow and pressure, the greater the generating capacity. **10.** If the orifice were larger, water would exit faster. If the orifice were smaller, water would exit more slowly. **11.** A gate or sluice used in controlling the flow of water. A tube or trough for carrying water to a water wheel, or a pipe carrying water to an electric turbine. Students' sentences will vary. **12.** Valves placed in water lines can be used to open or close the lines. This can increase or decrease water pressure.

Activity: Distillation and Desalination: Fresh Water From Salt Water
Critical Thinking and Application
1. distilled water **2.** Salt has been removed. **3.** minerals and salts **4.** It helped the water condense quickly. **5.** Yes, an abundance of surface minerals and salts. **6.** desert areas **7.** process in the overall cycle **8.** It could be a source of fresh water.

Activity: Wise Use of Fresh Water
1. steady increase **2.** increased population and increased activities **3.** irrigation **4.** approximately 7200 million gallons

5. Answers will vary. **6.** Water is necessary to plants and animals for maintaining life. **7.** physical, chemical, and biological condition **8.** 7 **9.** sewage, paper manufacturing wastes **10.** water supplies, recreation, and fisheries **11.** thermal pollution **12.** ammonia, mercury, lead **13.** Pesticides and herbicides may enhance crop and animal production. Pesticides and herbicides may kill crops, other plants, and animals.

Laboratory Investigation: Porosity of Various Soils
Observations **1.** Students will find that the gravel holds the most water. **2.** Students will discover that the clay holds the least water. **Analysis and Conclusions** **1.** The amount of water that can be held in soil depends on how large each of the individual soil particles is. **2.** Students should conclude that porosity is determined by the size of individual soil particles. Therefore, the gravel will hold the most water, sand the next, the mixture the next, and clay the least. **3.** To compare the soil samples in this investigation with soil found on the school grounds, students would obtain three soil samples from three different places on the school grounds. Using a small trowel, they would fill each of three cups about three-fourths full with the soil samples. They then would follow steps 2 and 3 for each of the soil types. In general, the type of soil on the school grounds varies from one location to another. Soil from eroded areas will contain more clay and sand, whereas areas near plants will be more porous. **4.** Students should conclude that the roots of plants help to prevent erosion and, therefore, the soil near plants would be more porous than soil in eroded areas. Hypotheses and experimental designs will vary.

Contents

*Appropriate for cooperative learning

Chapter Discovery

Mapping an Outdoor Area

Materials
meterstick
ruler
colored pencils
9 small rocks
red and yellow paint
compass
sheet of unlined white paper

Preparation
Paint eight small rocks yellow and one small rock red before you carry out this activity.
Set the rocks aside to dry. You will use the rocks as markers in steps 2 and 3 of the
Procedure.

Procedure
Part A   Measuring and Observing
  1. Find an outdoor area that you can measure and walk in easily. Some possible areas
     include a large backyard, a portion of a park, a small pond and the surrounding
     land, part of a baseball or football field, part of a city street, a portion of your school
     grounds, or a section of a parking lot. **CAUTION:** *If the area you choose is not a public
     place, make sure that you have permission to be there.*

  2. Mark the boundaries of the area you intend to use by placing the yellow rocks as
     markers. Try to arrange the rocks in a shape that is easy to draw and measure, such
     as a rectangle.

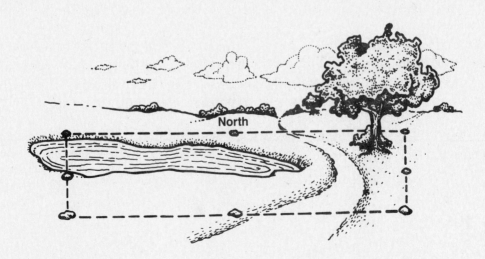

3. Stand in the center of the area you have marked off and use the compass to locate north. Note where the arrow of the compass is pointing and walk to this place on the edge of your space. Place the red rock there as a marker to indicate the north side of your area.

4. Stand on the other side of your area directly opposite the north side. Make a sketch of your area on a separate piece of paper. Make sure that the north side of your area is at the top of the page. Draw a symbol in the upper corner of the page to show North–South–East–West.

5. Using the meterstick, measure each side of your area. Record the measurements on your sketch.

6. Now look at the features within your area. For example, if you are in a park, you might see trees, benches, a small pond, a seesaw. If you are on a city street you might see buildings, a traffic sign, a fire hydrant, or a vendor's cart. Indicate on your sketch the location of each feature. (*For now, just write lightly in pencil. You may want to make changes later.*) If there are many features, choose several of the most interesting ones.

7. Observe the ground surface of your area. Is there more than one type of surface? For example, is part of the area grass, and another part pavement? Indicate on your drawing the various ground surfaces.

8. Is the ground in your area level? Or is there a slope? Is there a bump or a ditch? Indicate on your drawing any changes in the level of your area.

Part B Making Your Map
1. Look at the dimensions of the area you drew. Based on these dimensions, choose a scale for your map. The scale should make your map fit easily onto a sheet of unlined white paper. However, make sure you leave enough white space around the

map to place a legend and a scale. Record your scale here: _____

_____

2. Decide on symbols to represent the various features—trees, buildings, and so forth—in your area. Record the symbols you have chosen here:

_____

_____

3. Decide on a way to show the various ground surfaces in your area. For example, you may wish to make each surface a different color. Record the way you will show

various ground surfaces here: _____

_____

_____

4. If your area has uneven ground, decide how you will show differences in level. One possible way is by shading; for example, darker shading for lower elevations, lighter shading for higher elevations. Record how you will show different levels in your area:

_____

_____

_____

5. Use the scale you have chosen to draw an outline of your area on a sheet of unlined white paper. Remember to place the north side of your area at the top of the page. Draw a North–South–East–West symbol in an upper corner of your map.

6. Fill in your area to show the various ground surfaces and different elevations. Use the methods you chose in steps 3 and 4.

7. Place symbols on your map to show the various features in your area. Use the symbols you chose in step 2.

8. Near the bottom of the page, draw a legend to show the meaning of your symbols and the methods you chose to indicate ground surfaces and elevation. Also make a drawing of your scale.

9. Give your map a title. Your map is done!

Critical Thinking and Application

1. Which step in the map-making process did you find the most difficult? Why?

_____

_____

2. Which step did you find the easiest or most enjoyable? Why?

_____

_____

3. Suppose you had to make a map of a much larger area. What additional problems might you encounter?

_____

_____

4. Based on your experiences in this activity, what are some of the challenges of mapmaking? Do you appreciate the skill of mapmaking more now that you have made a map of your own?

_____

_____

Activity

Latitude, Longitude, and Time Zones

Part A   Latitude and Longitude

Any experienced sailor or pilot knows the importance of latitude and longitude when navigating. In this activity you will practice using latitude and longitude coordinates.

Determine the latitude and longitude coordinates for the numbered locations on the world map. Then enter the coordinates in the appropriate space in Data Table 1. Make sure you label each coordinate as North, South, East, or West.

Now place a point on the map for each location identified by the latitude and longitude coordinates in Data Table 2. Print the appropriate location letter next to each point to identify it.

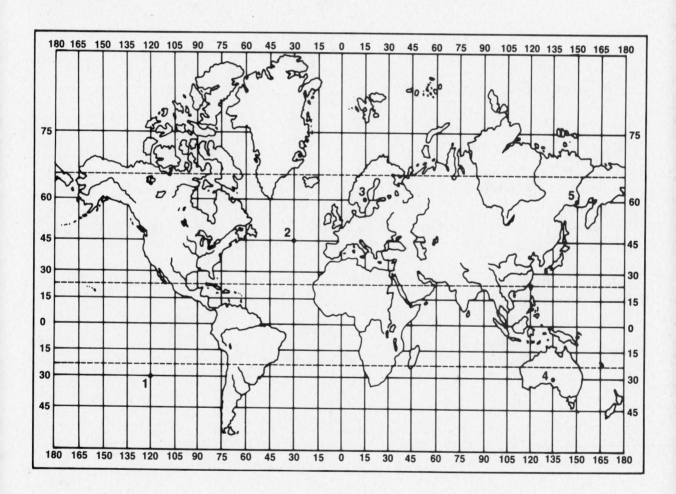

Data Table 1

Location	Latitude	Longitude
1		
2		
3		
4		
5		

Data Table 2

Location	Latitude	Longitude
A	15° S	150° W
B	0°	60° E
C	75° N	45° W
D	45° S	105° E
E	15° N	30° E

Part B Time Zones

A day is 24 hours long, as you know. During these 24 hours, the Earth rotates 15° every hour. The Earth is divided into 24 time zones of 15° of longitude each. A time zone is a longitudinal belt of the Earth in which the local time is the same.

When you cross from one time zone to another, the local time changes by one hour. If you are traveling east, you add one hour for each time zone you cross. If you are traveling west, you subtract one hour.

Using the world map, determine the time zones and the time at locations 2 to 5 if it is 8:00 PM at location 1. Write your answers in Data Table 3.

Data Table 3

Location	Time Zone (° longitude)	Time
1	120° W	8 PM
2		
3		
4		
5		

Identifying Our Planet's Most Noticeable Features

If you were a traveler approaching the Earth from outer space, you would be impressed with the fact that the Earth appears to be mostly covered with ocean water, separated here and there by huge landmasses called continents. Upon closer examination, an observer would notice that there were also smaller landmasses called islands as well as smaller bodies of water called seas and lakes. In this activity you will be asked to correctly identify some of the larger landmasses and bodies of water that are most noticeable on the global scale. These features help to distinguish our world as planet Earth.

The following table lists several names of physical features such as continents, islands, oceans, and seas. A map of the world also has been provided, which shows the general size and position of major landmasses and bodies of water.

Continents	Oceans	Seas	Islands
Africa	North Atlantic	Mediterranean	Cuba
Antarctica	South Atlantic	Red	Greenland
North America	Arctic		Japan
South America	Indian		Madagascar
Asia	Pacific		New Guinea
Australia			New Zealand
Europe			

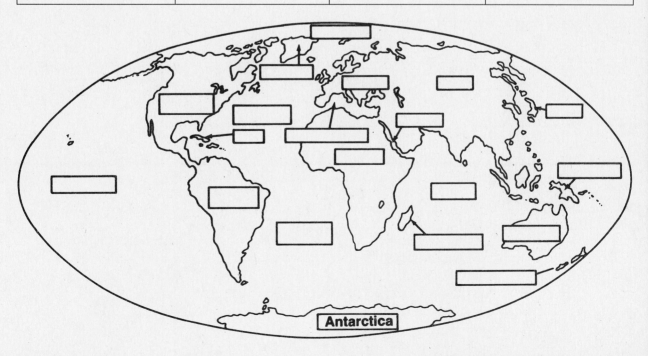

Study the information found in the table. From this list, write the name of the body of water or landmass in the proper box on the world map. Notice that one example has been completed for you—the continent of Antarctica has been labeled in the box provided. Check the map for this example.

After you have written the names of each of the features listed in the table in the proper boxes on the map, color in all of the continents using a different color for each. Be sure to color around the boxes containing the names of the features. You may use crayons or colored pencils, selecting colors of your choice.

After you have completed the map, answer these questions.

1. How many continents have been listed and identified?

_____

2. How many oceans did you label and what are their names?

_____

3. List the names of at least three islands shown on the map.

_____

4. Name the continent on which you live.

_____

5. a. Which is the largest continent?

_____

   b. Which is the largest ocean?

_____

   c. Which is the largest island?

_____

Activity

CHAPTER
4

An Island Trip

A boy spending a vacation on a small island wrote to his sister. He wanted to tell her about a bike trip he had taken. Here is part of the letter.

"The town where we are staying is in the center of the island. There is a road from the town that leads to a deserted village on the shore of the island. Yesterday we decided to go there on our bikes. On the way out of town we came to a fork in the road by a tall tree. We went to the right. And, as you can guess, the road to the village was the one on the left. Anyway, we were lost.

"After a while we came to a four-way intersection. We were not sure if we should keep going straight ahead, turn left, or turn right. We decided to turn right and soon came to a forest. (Later we found out that the road to the left leads to a nice beach. Going straight ahead would have taken us to some cliffs overlooking the ocean.)

"Soon we came to another fork in the road and decided to go left. (We should have turned right. That would have taken us back to town.) We ended up at the boat dock on the other side of the island. By then we were tired, so we wanted to go back to town. We knew there was a direct road from the boat dock to town, but we missed it. Instead we ended up going along the shore of the island all the way to the deserted village. So we visited the village after all, but we sure went the long way.

"What I don't understand is how we got to the village from the dock and never crossed any other roads. After all, the village and the dock are almost on opposite ends of the island."

His sister couldn't make head or tail out of the description of her brother's trip. So, she decided to draw a sketch of the island, its roads, and its landmarks.

1. In the space provided, draw a sketch of the island and the trip using the description given in the letter.

2. Compare your sketch with your classmates' sketches. In what ways are they alike? In what ways are they different?

_____

_____

_____

_____

_____

_____

Reprinted by permission of Uri Haber-Schaim *et al.* from *Mathematics 1,* Prentice-Hall, © 1980

Activity

Science Concentration

Science Concentration can be played with one or two friends. Before beginning the game, cut out the vocabulary word cards and the definition cards. After you have done this, shuffle all the cards and place them singly face down on a table or desk.

To start the game, a player turns over two cards, one at a time. If these two cards contain a vocabulary word and its correct definition, that player scores one point and the cards are removed from the playing area. If the cards do not match, they are returned to their original positions.

Another player then turns over two cards, one at a time. Again, cards are removed from the playing area only if a vocabulary word matches its definition. Players continue to take turns until all the vocabulary words have been matched with their definitions. The player with the most points wins the game.

island	shield
topography	landscape
relief	coastal plains

interior plains	longitude

latitude	elevation

plateau	continent

a small land area completely surrounded by water	area of very old rock

shape of the Earth's surface	different physical features of the Earth's surface in an area

differences in height among
landforms in a particular
area

low, flat areas along a coast

measure of distance north
and south of the equator

measure of distance east
and west of the prime meridian

broad, flat areas of land
over 600 m above sea level

large landmass on the Earth

height above sea level

low, flat areas
inland on the continents

Activity

Mountain Ranges

The Himalayas, Alps, Rockies, Sierra Nevadas, Cascades, Appalachians, Urals, and Pyrenees are some of the mountain ranges of the world. Using reference materials in the library, find the location of each mountain range, its approximate length, and its highest peak. Write the information in the chart below.

Mountain Range	Location	Length	Greatest Height
Himalayas			
Alps			
Rockies			
Sierra Nevadas			
Cascades			
Appalachians			
Urals			
Pyrenees			

Activity

Earth's Landmasses

Identifying Landscape Regions
of the United States

The continental portions of the Earth's surface are generally classified into three major landscape types, depending on the physical characteristics of surface features and the underlying rock structure. The following table summarizes these landscape types.

Landscape Type	Landscape Characteristics
Plains	Plains are large areas that are flat, or nearly flat. Erosion may have produced differences in height between locations on a plain but the differences are only a few meters at most.
Plateaus	Plateaus, like plains, are large flat, or nearly flat, regions. However, erosion causes differences between the highest and lowest points on a plateau to be much greater than for a plain. As an example, the difference between the top and bottom of the Grand Canyon on the Colorado Plateau is almost 1.5 kilometers.
Mountains	Mountains are parts of the Earth's crust in which the rock layers are not horizontal. They may be bent or broken and often contain igneous rock. Mountains may consist of one or more volcanoes. Usually the difference in height between the lowest and highest points in a mountainous region can be measured in thousands of meters.

The next table lists the main landscape regions for the continental United States. Each region is classified as representing an area of plains, plateaus, or mountains. These same landscape regions are outlined and numbered on the map. Numbers 1, 3, 6, 8, and 11 are mountains. Numbers 2, 5, and 7 are plateaus. Numbers 4, 9, and 10 are plains. Correctly identify each of the landscape regions on the map by labeling them in the spaces provided. You will need to refer to a map of the United States that shows the names of plains, plateaus, and mountains in order to locate some of these regions.

Landscape Type	Main Landscape Regions
Mountains	Pacific Mountain System Rocky Mountain System Ouachita Mountains Appalachian Mountains Adirondack Mountains
Plateaus	Inter-Mountain Plateau Ozark Plateau Appalachian Plateau
Plains	Interior Plains Atlantic Coastal Plains Piedmont Plains

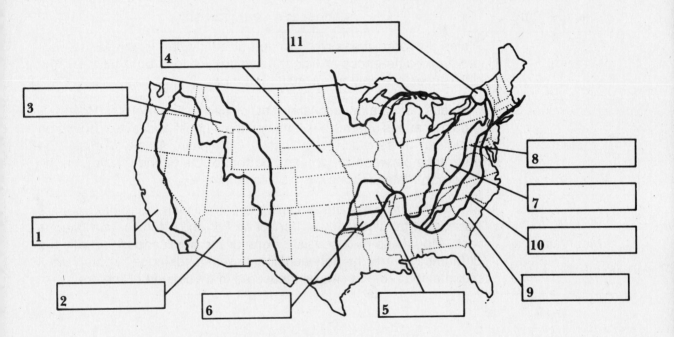

Answer the following questions after you have completed the map.

1. In which of the three main types of landscape regions do you live?

_____

2. What is the name of the landscape region in which you live?

_____

3. In what important way are mountainous landscape regions different from plains and plateaus?

_____

_____

4. Many major landscape regions can be further divided into smaller areas called geologic or physiographic provinces. Refer to a geology textbook to answer the following questions:

a. How are geologic or physiographic provinces different from the landscape regions that were identified in this activity?

_____

_____

_____

b. In which geologic or physiographic province do you live?

_____

Activity

Topographic Maps

People use different kinds of maps to find out different kinds of information. A topographic map is a flat map that can be used to show elevation. A mountain, for example, on a topographic map is drawn as a series of curved loops, one loop inside the other. Each loop is called a contour line. Each contour line passes through areas of equal elevation. In the drawing on the left below, a mountain is shown as it might appear on a topographic map. Notice that the first curved line is labeled 50, which in this case means an elevation of 50 meters. The intervals between each contour line on this contour map are 5 meters. So each line represents an elevation of 5 meters above the line just outside of it. In this case, there are 3 more contour lines inside the 50-meter line. The elevation of the peak of this mountain is 65 meters. Sometimes the contour lines have smaller lines extending inward. These lines indicate that the elevation is decreasing, not increasing. The drawing on the right, then, shows an area that has an elevation at its center of 35 meters.

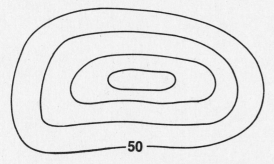
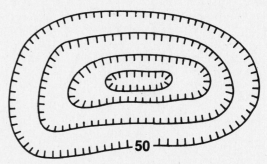

Use the topographic map included in this activity to answer the following questions.

1. What is the exact elevation of the following points?

   a. Point A = _____ meters   b. Point E = _____ meters

2. What is the approximate elevation of the following points?

   a. Point C = _____ meters   b. Point F = _____ meters

3. Explain why you can determine the exact elevation for points A and E but only approximate elevations for points C and F.

_____

_____

4. How many hills are shown on the map? _____

5. In which direction is the Ert River flowing? _____

6. Which of the following points have the same elevation? _____

   a. Points A and B   b. Points E and A   c. Points C and D   d. Points F and C

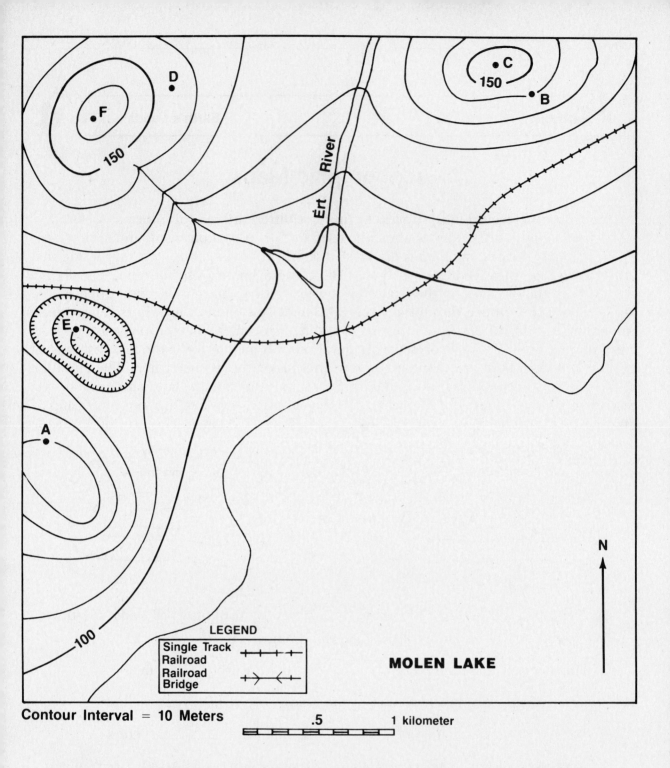

Contour Interval = 10 Meters

.5   1 kilometer

Now you are ready to try your hand at mapmaking. Using a pencil, draw the following in Molen Lake.

1. Draw an island approximately 1.5 km long and 1.0 km wide. Draw it in Molen Lake so that its longest dimension runs approximately north–south.

2. Add a mountain with an elevation between 120 and 130 meters to the northern end of the island. Draw a lake on top of the mountain with a river flowing out of it in an easterly direction.

3. Add a mountain that has a hole on its top that is between 10 and 20 meters deep on the southern end of the island.

4. Label all of the contour lines on the island in meters.

Activity

A Typical Topography

Much of the geology of an area is concerned with the activities that affect the Earth's surface. Wind, running water, groundwater, ice, vulcanism, and Earth movements continuously act on the surface of the state and produce many surface features.

By studying the landforms in an area, it is possible to determine what processes are at work now and what processes were at work in the past. The basic tool for this task is the topographic map. A topographic map represents a view of the landscape as seen from above. The map is a scale drawing that shows various details of landforms—size, shape, and relative distances among them. Figure 1 shows examples of typical landforms. Figure 2 is a corresponding topographic map.

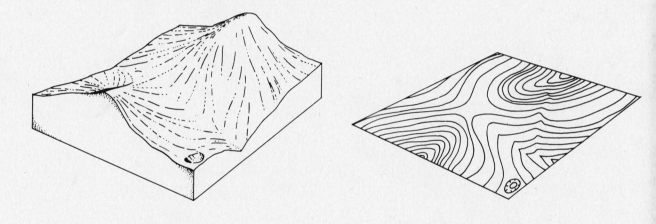

Figure 1   **Figure 2**

The full-page topographic map in Figure 3 is of the small town of Damon. Highway 36 runs northwest to southeast on the east side of town. The surrounding countryside is flat and devoid of contrasting landforms. Damon is built on a mound that consists of about 1200 hectares. Northwest of the mound, beginning almost at the base, lies a wooded area and a limestone quarry.

The mound itself is caused by a massive dome of salt that is slowly working its way from deep beneath Damon to the surface of the Earth. The contour lines, or curved lines on the map, connect points of equal elevation. High areas are represented by a series of roughly circular contour lines. As the elevation increases, the circles become smaller. Closely spaced lines represent steep slopes. Lines farther apart represent gentle slopes. The change in elevation between lines is 1.5 meters (5 feet). Use the topographic map to answer the following questions about the surface features of Damon Mound. Remember, you will need to convert to metric units to answer the questions.

Exploring Planet Earth I ∎ **131**

Figure 3 Topographic Map of Damon

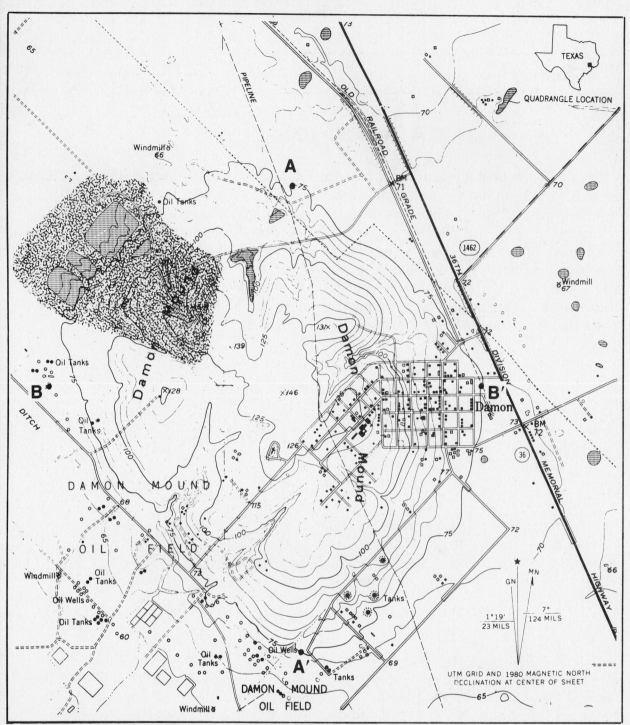

Source: U.S. Department of the Interior.

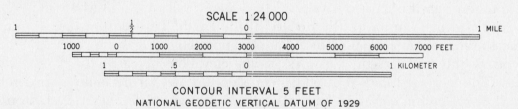

SCALE 1:24 000

CONTOUR INTERVAL 5 FEET
NATIONAL GEODETIC VERTICAL DATUM OF 1929

1. What is the lowest elevation shown on the map? _____ What is the highest elevation on the mound? _____ Based on these values, how high is Damon Mound? _____

2. A cemetery, marked with a cross, is located on top of the mound. What is its elevation? _____

3. Oil is produced at the mound. In what direction from the mound is the oil field located? _____

4. Does Damon Mound appear to cross Highway 36? _____

5. Compare the closeness of the contour lines on the west side of the mound with those on the east side of the mound. Which side shows the steepest slope?

   _____

6. Study the top of the mound. How would you describe its appearance? _____

   _____

   _____

7. Houses appear on the map as small black squares. Is housing found throughout the entire area of the mound? _____

8. Oil wells appear as small white circles. Where are most of the wells at Damon Mound found? _____

   _____

9. What is the north-south distance (A A′) of Damon Mound? _____ The west-east distance (B B′)? _____

   It is often desirable to construct a profile, or cross section, of landforms. A profile gives a more natural view of an area and shows hills and valleys from the side. You will now construct a profile of Damon Mound from point A to point A′. Use the following directions and Figure 4 to make your profile.

1. Place a strip of paper along line A A′ as shown in Figure 4a. On the paper, mark the exact spot where each contour line crosses the strip. Label the elevation of each line.

2. Place the paper strip along the bottom of the chart as shown in Figure 4b. Transfer each mark on the paper strip to the proper spot on Figure 5.

3. Connect all the points with a smooth line.

Exploring Planet Earth I ■ 133

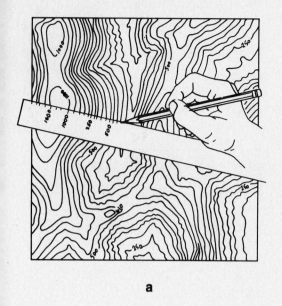

a

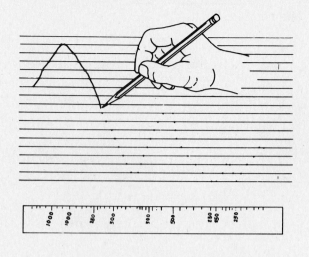

b

Figure 4

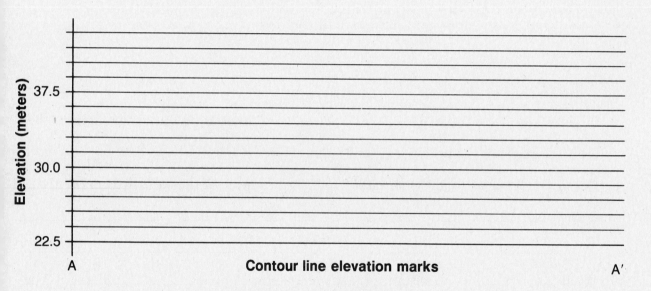

Figure 5   Damon Mound Profile

_____ *Laboratory Investigation* _____

CHAPTER 4 ■ Earth's Landmasses

Making a Topographic Map

Problem

What information can a topographic map provide about the surface features of the Earth?

Materials *(per group)*

modeling clay   glass-marking pencil
metric ruler   1 L water
rigid cardboard   pencil
pane of clear glass   sheet of unlined,
aquarium tank or   white paper
   deep-sided pan

Procedure 🔺

1. Cut the cardboard to fit the bottom of the tank or pan.
2. On top of the cardboard, shape the clay into a model of a hill. Include on the model some gullies, a steep slope, and a gentle slope.
3. When the model is dry and hard, place the model and cardboard into the tank or pan. Pour water into the container to a depth of 1 cm. This will represent sea level.
4. Place the pane of glass over the container. Looking straight down into the container, use the glass-marking pencil to trace the outline of the container on the glass. Also trace on the glass the contour, or outline, of the water around the edges of the model. Carefully remove the pane of glass from the container.
5. Add another centimeter of water to the container. The depth of the water should now be 2 cm. Place the glass in exactly the same position as before. Trace the new contour of the water on the pane of glass.

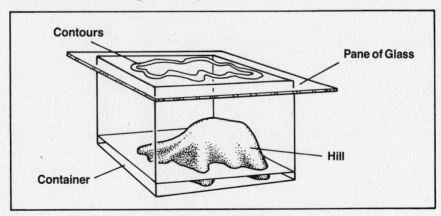

6. Repeat step 5, adding 1 cm to the depth of the water each time. Stop when the next addition of water would completely cover the model.

7. Remove the pane of glass. With a pencil, trace the contours on the glass onto a sheet of paper. This will be your topographic map.

8. Assume that every centimeter of water you added to the first centimeter (sea level) equals 100 m of elevation on the map. Label the elevation of each contour line on your topographic map.

Observations

1. What is the approximate elevation of the top of the hill?

_____

2. How can you determine if the hill has a steep slope by looking at the contour lines?

_____

_____

3. How can you determine if the hill has a gentle slope by looking at the contour lines?

_____

_____

4. How do contour lines look when they show gullies on the model?

_____

_____

Analysis and Conclusions

1. What information can a topographic map provide about the Earth's surface?

_____

_____

_____

_____

Answer Key

Chapter Discovery: Mapping an Outdoor Area

Part B 1. and 2 Answers will vary. **Critical Thinking and Application** **1.** and **2.** Accept all reasonable answers. **3.** Possible answers include: measuring the area, observing the area carefully, and selecting a scale. **4.** Accept all reasonable answers.

Activity: Latitude, Longitude, and Time Zones

Part A. Data Table 1: **1** 30°S, 120°W **2** 45°N, 30°W **3** 60°N, 15°E **4** 30°S, 135°E **5** 60°N, 150°E **Part B. Data Table 3:** **2** 30°W, 2:00 PM **3** 15°E, 11:00 AM **4** 135°E, 3:00 AM **5** 150°E, 2:00 AM

Activity: Identifying Our Planet's Most Noticeable Features

1. Seven **2.** Five: North Atlantic, South Atlantic, Arctic, Pacific, Indian **3.** See table for names of the six islands listed on the map. **4.** North America **5.** a. Asia b. Pacific c. Greenland

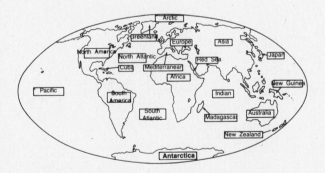

Problem-Solving Activity: An Island Trip

Sketches will vary but should include all the roads and landmarks included in the letter.

Activity: Science Concentration

island: a small land area completely surrounded by water **topography:** shape of the Earth's surface **relief:** differences in height among landforms in a particular area **interior plains:** low, flat areas inland on the continents **latitude:** measure of distance north and south of the equator **shield:** area of very old rock **landscape:** different physical features of the Earth's surface in an area **coastal plains:** low, flat areas along a coast **longitude:** measure of distance east and west of the prime meridian **plateau:** broad, flat areas of land over 600 meters above sea level **elevation:** height above sea level **continent:** large landmass on the Earth

Activity: Mountain Ranges

By using reference materials in the library, students should be able to complete the chart with the following information. **Himalayas:** from Afghanistan south through Kasmir and southern Tibet to northern Burma; 2400 km; Mount Everest 8854 m **Alps:** from southern France east through Switzerland and northern Italy to Austria; 1120 km; Mont Blanc 4810 m **Rockies:** from Alaska south through Canada and the U.S. to Mexico; 3520 km; Mount McKinley 6194 m **Sierra-Nevadas:** along the border of California and Nevada; 640 km; Mount Whitney 4418 m **Cascades:** from northern California north through Oregon and Washington into Canada; 1000 km; Mount Rainier 4392 m **Appalachians:** from Alabama north to eastern Canada; 2400 km; Mount Mitchell 2013 m **Urals:** along the division between Europe and Asia in the U.S.S.R.; 2000 km; Mount Narodnaya 1895 m **Pyrenees:** along the border between France and Spain; 384 km; Pico de Aneto 3406 m

Activity: Identifying Landscape Regions of the United States

1. Pacific Mountain System **2.** Inter-Mountain System **3.** Rocky Mountain System **4.** Interior Plains **5.** Ozark Plateau **6.** Ouachita Mountains

7. Appalachian Plateau   **8.** Appalachian
Mountains   **9.** Atlantic Coastal Plains
10. Piedmont Plains   **11.** Adirondack
Mountains   **Questions   1** and **2.** Answers
will vary.   **3.** Rock layers in mountainous
regions are not horizontal; they are horizontal
in areas of plains or plateaus.   **4.**   a. The
rock structure and climate may vary
considerably within a landscape region, but
the designation of "geologic or physiographic
province" is more specific; therefore, the rock
structure and climate will be the same for the
entire geologic or physiographic province.
b. Answers will vary.

Problem-Solving Activity: Topographic Maps

1.   a. 140 m   b. 90 m   **2.**   a. between
150 m and 160 m   b. between 160 m and
170 m   **3.** Since points A and E are located
on a contour line, their exact elevation is
known. Since points C and F are not located
on a contour line, only their approximate
height can be determined; their elevation is
between the value of the next highest contour
line and the next lowest.   **4.** Three
5. South   **6.** a

Problem-Solving Activity: A Typical Topography

1. 18 m   43.8 m   25.8 m   **2.** 39 m
3. Southwest   **4.** No.   **5.** Westside   **6.** The
top is covered with several small mounds
separated by ditches that drop down to the
base of the mound.   **7.** No.   **8.** Around the
low outer edges of the mound   **9.** 4.1 km
3.95 km   **Damon Mound Profile** Check
diagrams for accuracy.

Laboratory Investigation: Making a Topographic Map

Observations   1. Answers will vary,
depending on the model students
construct.   **2.** The contour lines will be close
together.   **3.** The contour lines will be
spaced farther apart.   **4.** The contour lines
have a slight V-shaped indent where they
cross the gully.   **Analysis and Conclusions**
1. Students should conclude that topographic
maps can show the shapes and sizes of
landscape features. Topographic maps also
show the land's relief using contour lines.

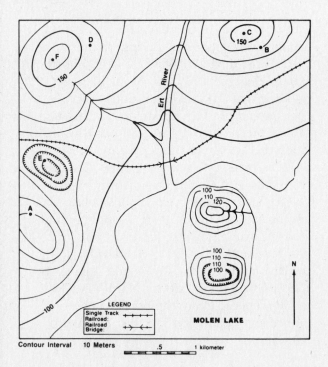

Contents

*Appropriate for cooperative learning

Exploring the Earth's Interior

How much do you know about the Earth's interior? How much do you think you know? This activity will test your knowledge. The diagram below shows the layers of the Earth's interior. Following the diagram is a list of facts. Your job is to match the facts in each category to the correct layer of the Earth. You may not use all the facts in each category, and some you may use more than once. After you have finished, put your diagram aside until you have studied Chapter 5 in your textbook. Then check yourself to see how much you knew.

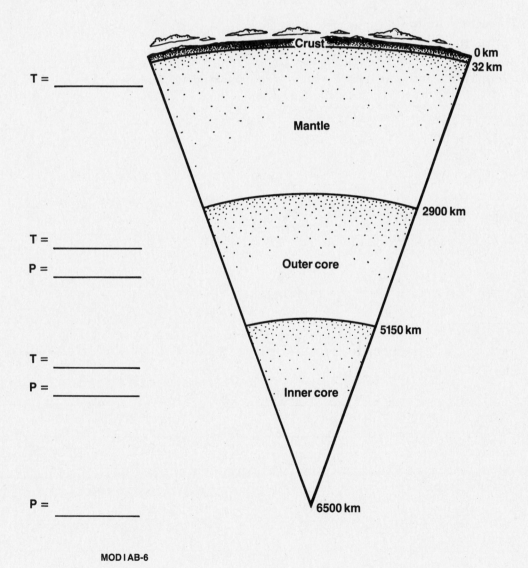

MOD I AB-6

Fact Set A: States of Matter
solid
liquid
plastic (flowing solid)
gas

Fact Set B: Temperature
870°C
2200°C
5000°C

Fact Set C: Density
3.3–5.5 g/cm³
11.5 g/cm³
9.5–11.5 g/cm³
2.7 g/cm³

Fact Set D: Major Elements
silicon and oxygen
iron and nickel
silicon, oxygen, aluminum, calcium, sodium, and potassium

Fact Set E: Pressure
3.75 million atmospheres
1.5 million atmospheres
3.25 million atmospheres

Critical Thinking and Application

1. What do you think happens to pressure as you move from the Earth's surface to the center? Why?

_____

_____

2. What do you think happens to temperature as you move from the Earth's surface to the center? Why?

_____

_____

_____

3. What do you think happens to density as you move from the surface of the Earth to the center? Why?

_____

_____

4. List at least two facts about the inner Earth that you would like to learn.

_____

_____

5. No one has ever explored the inner Earth directly. Can you think of a reason for this?

_____

_____

Activity _____ Earth's Interior CHAPTER **5**

Richter Scale

The Richter scale is used to measure the strength of an earthquake. Use the information in the table to answer the questions on the reverse of this page.

Magnitude	Strength (10 × as great as previous magnitude)	Results
1	0	Not felt by people; no damage to structures
2	10	Not felt by people; no damage to structures
3	100	Felt by people; some rattling of windows and dishes
4	1000	Slight damage to structures
5	10,000	Minor quake; some damage to structures
6	100,000	Some damage to reinforced concrete; severe damage to adobe houses; breakage of windows, dishes, and glassware
7	1,000,000	Severe damage to structures; damage extending 10 kilometers from epicenter; cracks in ground
8	10,000,000	"Great" quake; total destruction near epicenter; large chunks of landscape moved out of place; severe damage extending 20 kilometers from epicenter; damage extending 200 kilometers

Exploring Planet Earth I ■ 145

1. At what number on the Richter scale is an earthquake strong enough to be felt by people?

_____

_____

2. How many times greater in strength is an earthquake rated 4 on the Richter scale than an earthquake rated 2?

_____

_____

3. At what number on the Richter scale does an earthquake cause severe damage to structures?

_____

_____

4. Observations of an earthquake's effects show severe damage to buildings, cracks in the ground, and damage extending 10 km from the epicenter. What rating on the Richter scale would this earthquake most likely receive?

_____

_____

5. How many times increase in strength does each increase in magnitude on the Richter scale represent?

_____

_____

Layers of the Earth

Identify the layers of the Earth and their average thicknesses.

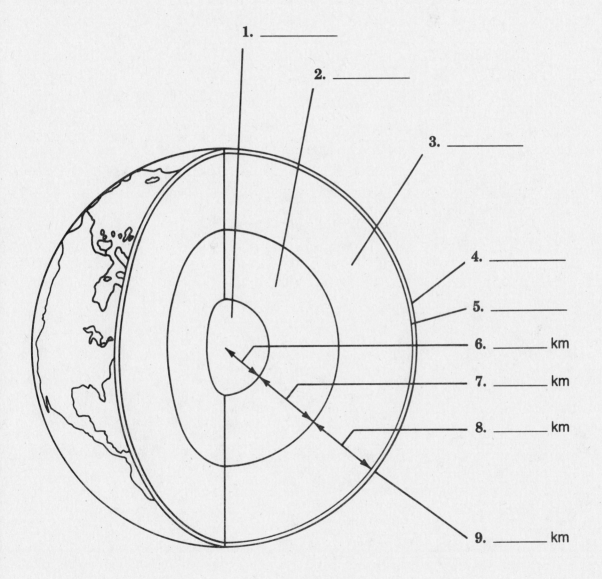

1. _____

2. _____

3. _____

4. _____

5. _____

6. _____ km

7. _____ km

8. _____ km

9. _____ km

Activity

The Earth's Interior

Scientists use earthquake waves to investigate the internal structure of the Earth in much the same way that a doctor uses X-rays to reveal information about the internal structure of a person.

The diagram summarizes information about the Earth's interior that has been inferred from the analysis of earthquake waves. Answer the following questions based on this diagram.

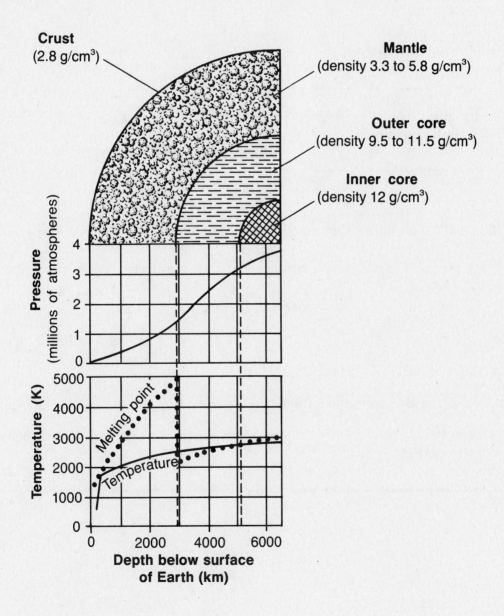

1. At what depth below the surface of the Earth does the outer core begin?

   _____

2. Approximately how thick is the outer core? _____

3. List the four layers of the Earth in order from the thickest layer to the thinnest layer.

   _____ thickest layer

   _____

   _____

   _____ thinnest layer

4. What is the temperature of the interior of the Earth at a depth of 1000 km?

   _____

5. At approximately what depth is the internal temperature of the Earth thought to be
   2500 K? _____

6. What information from the diagram supports the theory that the outer core of the
   Earth is in the liquid state?

   _____

   _____

7. What happens to the internal pressure of the Earth as depth below the surface
   increases? _____

8. What is the approximate density of crustal material? _____

9. In which of the four layers of the Earth would you be most likely to find Earth
   material with a density of 4.5 g/cm^3? _____

10. Which part of the Earth contains the densest material? _____

11. What is the relationship between the density of Earth materials and depth below the
    surface of the Earth?

    _____

Making a Scale Model of the Earth's Interior

Part A

Information gained from the study of earthquake waves that pass through the Earth's interior has helped scientists to develop a picture of what it may be like inside the Earth. In this activity you will make a scale model of the Earth that shows what the inside of the Earth would look like if you could cut it in half and examine the cut surface.

1. First calculate the width or thickness of the Earth's layers for your scale model. The four main layers of the Earth are listed in the Data Table that gives the thickness of each layer. Use the following formula to calculate the thickness of each layer on your scale model. Enter the values in the appropriate spaces provided in the Data Table. Be sure to round off all values to the nearest whole number.

DATA TABLE

Layer of the Earth	Thickness of Each Layer of the Earth	Thickness of Each Layer for the Scale Model
Crust	32 km	
Mantle	2900 km	
Outer core	2250 km	
Inner core	1300 km	

$$\text{Thickness of each layer for the scale model (mm)} = \frac{\text{thickness of each layer of the Earth (km)}}{70}$$

2. Using a drawing compass and a metric ruler, make a circle near the center of an unlined sheet of paper with a radius that is equal to the thickness of the inner core of your scale model. What does this circle represent? _____

_____

3. Increase the opening on your compass to equal the radius distance from the center of the scale model to the upper level of the outer core. Using this new radius, draw a circle around the inner core. What does this new layer represent? _____

_____

4. Repeat the above procedure to add the mantle and crust to your scale model. Label all four layers. Indicate on the diagram the actual thickness and the scale model thickness of each layer.

Part B

After you have completed your scale model, answer the following questions.

1. Many of the deepest earthquakes occur at approximately 700 km below the surface of the Earth. In which layer of the Earth do these deep earthquakes occur?

_____

2. a. What is the thickest layer of the Earth? _____

   b. What is the thinnest layer of the Earth? _____

3. If you were to use an apple as a scale model of the Earth, what part of the apple

   would approximately represent the Earth's crust? _____

4. All of the food, water, and natural resources that people need to survive on the Earth are provided by the crust. Why should we be very careful about how we use and take care of the Earth's crust? Write a short paragraph to answer this question.

_____

_____

_____

_____

_____

_____

_____

_____

Activity _____ Earth's Interior

How Does the Intensity of an Earthquake Change With Distance?

When an earthquake occurs, waves of energy spread outward in all directions from the point where the earthquake originated. As the waves pass through rock material, they cause the rock to shake or vibrate. The closer a person is to the point of origin, which is called the focus, the more noticeable the shaking becomes. At the location on the Earth's surface, directly above the earthquake's focus, great damage and terrible destruction sometimes take place. This location is called the epicenter. Farther away, less damage occurs.

Earth scientists have developed "scales of intensity" that describe the kinds of experiences that people share during an earthquake, depending on their distance from the earthquake's focus. One example of such a scale of intensity is shown below. Notice that this scale, called the Rossi–Forel Scale of Earthquake Intensity, ranges from I to X. Earthquake intensities of I are the least noticeable, while those labeled X are the most intense.

Rossi–Forel Scale of Earthquake Intensity

I. Recorded by instruments; felt only by experienced observers at rest.

II. Felt by small number of persons at rest.

III. Felt by several persons at rest; strong enough for the duration or direction to be appreciable.

IV. Felt by several persons in motion; disturbance of movable objects, doors, windows; creaking of floors.

V. Felt generally by everyone; disturbance of furniture and beds; ringing of some bells.

VI. General awakening of those asleep; general ringing of bells; oscillation of chandeliers; stopping of clocks; visible disturbance of trees and shrubs; some startled persons leave their dwellings.

VII. Overthrow of movable objects, fall of plaster, ringing of church bells, general panic, without damage to buildings.

VIII. Fall of chimneys, cracks in the walls of buildings.

IX. Partial or total destruction of some buildings.

X. Great disaster, ruins, disturbance of strata, fissures in the Earth's crust, rock-falls from mountains.

A description of one intensity level from this scale states that an earthquake of intensity IV would be "felt by several persons in motion . . . while movable objects such as doors and windows would be disturbed. Floors of houses would creak." At a different intensity level, people located in an intensity zone of IX would experience partial or total destruction of some of their buildings. Truly a frightening experience!

How would a severe earthquake affect people over a large region? On August 31, 1886, a devastating earthquake struck Charleston, South Carolina. The map illustrates the range of intensity of that earthquake as it was felt throughout the eastern part of the United States.

Observe the map carefully. Compare it to the Rossi–Forel scale of earthquake intensity. Answer the following questions that are based on both the map and the scale of earthquake intensity. Before you answer the questions, though, let's look at two examples that will help you to proceed. Charlotte, North Carolina, is a city about 300 km from Charleston and is inside the number VII earthquake intensity line. Therefore, people living in Charlotte at the time of the earthquake would probably have seen plaster fall, heard church bells ring, and have experienced general panic! However, most people living in the city of New Orleans, because they were located inside the number II earthquake intensity line, and nearly 1000 km away, would probably not even have felt the Charleston earthquake.

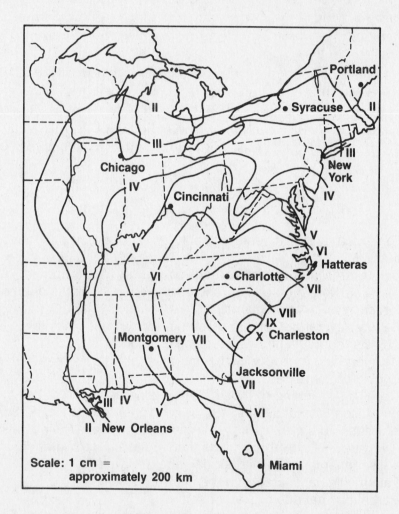

1. Name a city shown on the map in which the earthquake of August 31 was detected mainly by instruments, rather than by people.

_____

_____

2. Name two cities that suffered damage similar to Charleston but less severe.

_____

_____

3. a. What indication of the August 31 earthquake might a person have experienced in Chicago?

_____

b. How would their experiences have compared to those of people living in New York City?

_____

_____

4. Would people who were located 1000 km from Charleston generally have been awakened from their sleep as a result of the earthquake?

_____

_____

5. Describe the effect that the earthquake of August 31, 1886, had upon the city of Charleston, South Carolina.

_____

6. What general relationship seems to exist between earthquake intensity and distance from the earthquake center?

_____

7. a. Shade in the complete region where an earthquake would be felt by everyone, but where there would be no visible disturbance of trees and shrubs.

_____

b. Name at least two cities located in the zone referred to in a.

_____

Exploring Planet Earth I ■

Determining How Fast Some Crustal Plates Move

Most scientists believe that the Earth's crust is broken into pieces, much like the cracked shell of a hard-cooked egg. These pieces are called crustal plates and are thought to be moving across the mantle. The mantle is the layer of the Earth located directly under the crust.

The diagram illustrates how some scientists believe lines of volcanic islands are produced, as superheated molten material rises upward from deep within the mantle. The molten material breaks through weak places in the crustal plate as the plate moves over the stationary hot spot in the mantle. In the diagram, the first volcano is the oldest while the second and third get progressively younger. The fourth volcano is the youngest because it is still located over the hot spot in the mantle. Because volcanoes are formed in the ocean, they form what is referred to as a chain of volcanic islands, as their tops reach above the ocean surface.

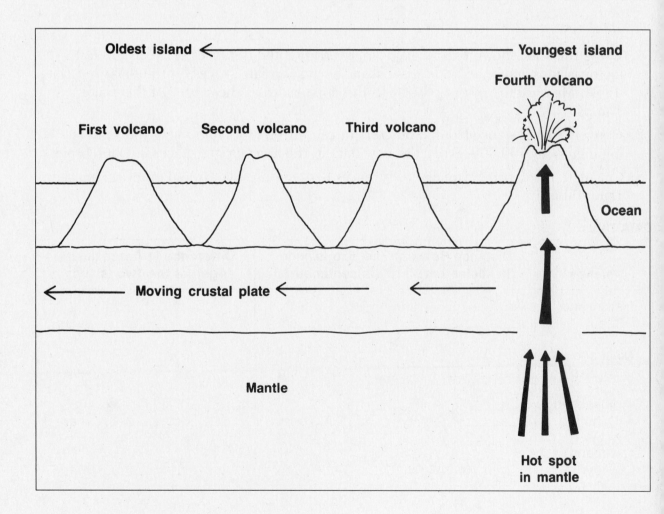

Using the idea that chains of volcanic islands are formed as a crustal plate moves over a hot spot in the mantle, it is possible to calculate the average speed at which the crustal plate is moving. The following diagram illustrates the eight main islands of the Hawaiian chain. The approximate age is given for the larger islands.

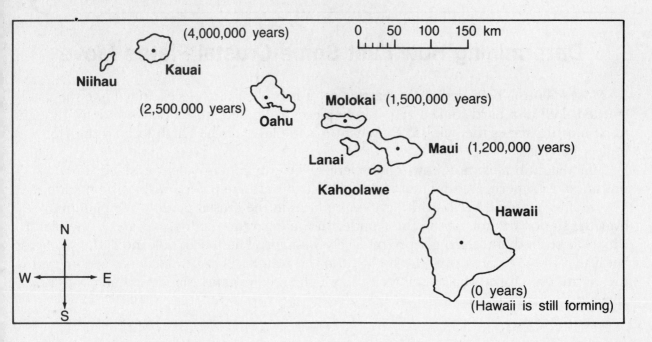

1. Using the scale shown on the diagram, determine the distances between the five major islands and enter your answers in the appropriate spaces on the following Data Table. Measure the distance between the dots placed at the center of the major islands.

2. Convert each distance from kilometers to centimeters by multiplying the value in kilometers by 100,000. Enter the new data in the appropriate spaces in Data Table 1.

3. Calculate the approximate age differences between the islands and enter the data in Data Table 1.

DATA TABLE 1

Islands	Distance Between the Two Islands (In kilometers)	(In centimeters)	Difference in Approximate Ages of the Two Islands
Hawaii and Maui	_____ km	_____ cm	_____ years
Maui and Molokai	_____ km	_____ cm	_____ years
Molokai and Oahu	_____ km	_____ cm	_____ years
Oahu and Kauai	_____ km	_____ cm	_____ years

4. Using the following formula, calculate the approximate speed at which the crustal plate was moving between the times that each of the islands formed. Enter your data in Data Table 2.

$$\frac{\text{Speed of crustal}}{\text{movement (cm/yr)}} = \frac{\text{Distance between the two islands (in centimeters)}}{\text{Difference in approximate ages of the two islands (in years)}}$$

DATA TABLE 2

Islands	Approximate Speed of Crustal Movement Between the Times That the Two Islands Formed (cm/yr)
Hawaii and Maui	_____ centimeters per year
Maui and Molokai	_____ centimeters per year
Molokai and Oahu	_____ centimeters per year
Oahu and Kauai	_____ centimeters per year

5. Now calculate the average speed of crustal movement.

Average speed of crustal movement = _____ centimeters per year.

After completing this activity, answer the following questions:

1. a. In which direction was the crustal plate apparently moving during the time that the Hawaiian Islands were formed? _____

_____

b. Explain your answer. _____

_____

2. a. According to your data, did the crustal plate always move at the same speed? _____

b. Explain your answer. _____

_____

Laboratory Investigation

Simulating Plasticity

Problem

How can the plasticity of the Earth's mantle be simulated?

Materials *(per group)*

15 g cornstarch
2 small beakers
10 mL cold water
medicine dropper
metal stirring rod or spoon

Procedure 🔺

1. Put 15 g of cornstarch in one of the beakers. Into the other beaker, pour 10 mL of cold water.

2. Use the medicine dropper to gradually add one dropperful of water to the cornstarch. Stir the mixture.

3. Continue to add the water, one dropperful at a time. Stir the mixture after each addition. Stop adding the water when the mixture becomes difficult to stir.

4. Try to pour the mixture into your hand. Try to roll the mixture into a ball and press it.

Observations

1. Before the addition of water, is the cornstarch a solid, liquid, or gas? Is the water a solid, liquid, or gas?

_____

2. When you try to pour the mixture into your hand, does the mixture behave like a solid, liquid, or gas?

_____

3. When you try to roll the mixture into a ball and apply pressure, does the mixture act like a solid, liquid, or gas?

_____

Analysis and Conclusions

1. How is the mixture of cornstarch and water similar to the Earth's mantle? Different from the Earth's mantle?

_____

_____

_____

2. How might the plasticity of the mantle influence the movement of the Earth's lithospheric plates?

_____

_____

_____

3. **On Your Own** Make a model of a lithospheric plate. Devise a way to show how the plasticity of the mantle allows the Earth's lithospheric plates to move.

Answer Key

Chapter Discovery: Exploring the Earth's Interior

Critical Thinking and Application

1. Increases, because of the weight of matter pressing down. **2.** Increases, possible reasons include: the increase in pressure causes an increase in temperature; breakdown of radioactive elements within the Earth produces heat causing a temperature increase in the Earth's interior. **3.** Increases, because of the pressure of matter being pushed together. **4.** Accept all reasonable answers. **5.** Accept all reasonable answers. Students will probably realize that the temperature and pressure of the inner Earth are too great to permit human exploration.

Activity: Richter Scale

1. 3 **2.** 100 times greater **3.** 7
4. 7 **5.** 10

Activity: Layers of the Earth

1. inner core **2.** outer core **3.** mantle
4. crust **5.** Moho **6.** 1300 km **7.** 2250 km **8.** 2900 km **9.** 8–32 km

Problem-Solving Activity: The Earth's Interior

1. approximately 2900–3000 km **2.** 2200 km **3.** mantle, outer core, inner core, crust **4.** approximately 2000 K **5.** approximately 3000 km **6.** The diagram indicates that the temperature of Earth materials in the outer core is higher than the temperature necessary to melt the material. **7.** increases **8.** about 2.7 g/cm³ **9.** mantle **10.** inner core **11.** As the depth below the surface increases, the density of the Earth materials increases.

Problem-Solving Activity: Making a Scale Model of the Earth's Interior

Part A. **1.** Chart: 0.5 = 1.0 mm 41.4 = 41.0 mm 32.1 = 32.0 mm 18.6 = 19.0 mm Point out to students that rounding off

will exaggerate the thickness of the crust relative to the other layers. Actually the average thickness of the crust varies between 8 km and 32 km. The formula allows students to calculate the relative thickness of the Earth's layers on a scale model converted to millimeters from 1/70 the actual width in kilometers. **2.** the inner core of the scale model of the Earth's interior **3.** the outer core of the scale model of the Earth's interior **4.** Check students' diagrams. The relative thickness of the model's layers should correspond to the actual thickness of the Earth's layers shown on the diagram. **Part B.** **1.** mantle **2.** a. mantle b. crust **3.** the peel **4.** Answers will vary but should incorporate the concept that the crust is very thin by comparison with the Earth's other layers and that once the crust is damaged or used up, there is no place to look for a replacement.

Problem-Solving Activity: How Does the Intensity of an Earthquake Change With Distance?

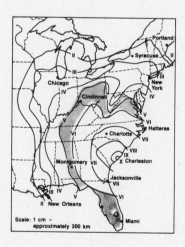

1. Any city outside the number II intensity line. The only city on the map is Portland, Maine. **2.** Cities in zones VII, VIII, and IX. Charlotte and Jacksonville in zone VII. No cities listed in zones VIII and IX. **3.** a. Chicago is located in zone III. People there would have barely felt the earthquake. b. New York City is also located in zone III. People there would have had the same experience as in Chicago.   **4.** No. The distance is well beyond zone VI. People would have had to be within this zone in order to have been awakened.   **5.** Charleston is within zone X. See intensity scale for effects within this zone.   **6.** As distance from the earthquake center increases, intensity decreases.   **7.**   a. The region would have been between intensity lines V and VI, that is, within zone V.   b. Cincinnati, Montgomery, and Miami.

Problem-Solving Activity: Determining How Fast Some Crustal Plates Move

Map Kauai and Oahu: 165 km; Oahu and Lanai: 110 km; Lanai and Maui: 80 km; Maui and Hawaii: 140 km   **Data Table 1** (across) **Row 1:** 140 km   14,000,000 cm   1,200,000 years   **Row 2:** 80 km   8,000,000 cm   300,000 years   **Row 3:** 110 km   11,000,000 cm   1,000,000 years   **Row 4:** 165 km   16,500,000 cm   1,500,000 years   **Data Table 2** (down) 11.7; 26.7; 11.0; 11.0 (All answers are centimeters per year.)   **5.**   12.4 cm/yr   495 km/4,000,000 yr = 49,500,000 cm/4,000,000 = 12.38 cm/yr   **1.**   a. From the southeast toward the northwest.   b. The position of the oldest volcano is to the northwest of the youngest one.   **2.** No. It varied from 11 cm/yr between Molokai and

Kauai to 26.7 cm/yr between Maui and Molokai.

Laboratory Investigation: Simulating Plasticity

Observations 1. Before the addition of water, cornstarch is a solid. The phase of the water is a liquid.   **2.** When pouring the mixture, it has the properties of a liquid.   **3.** When the mixture is rolled into a ball, it acts like a solid.   **Analysis and Conclusions 1.** The mixture has the property of plasticity, which is characteristic of the mantle. Students can see this happening when they roll the mixture into a ball and press it. The mixture, however, is not under intense heat and pressure.   **2.** Accept all logical responses. Because the plates move about on the mantle, a mantle that acted entirely like a solid would greatly impede the movement of the lithospheric plates. Plasticity, or the ability of a solid to flow like a liquid, greatly enhances the ability of the plates to move about atop the mantle. **3.** Students' models will vary. One possible experiment is as follows: Put jelly on top of a piece of cardboard that represents the asthenosphere. Use a piece of bread for the lithospheric plate. Put the bread layer on top of the jelly. Make a second model without the jelly. Place both models on a tray. Shake the tray sideways and note any movements of the bread.

Science Reading Skills

TO THE TEACHER

One of the primary goals of the *Prentice Hall Science* program is to help students acquire skills that will improve their level of achievement in science. Increasing awareness of the thinking processes associated with communicating ideas and reading content materials for maximum understanding are two skills students need in order to handle a more demanding science curriculum. Teaching reading skills to junior high school students at successive grade levels will help ensure the mastery of science objectives. A review of teaching patterns in secondary science courses shows a new emphasis on developing concept skills rather than on accumulating factual information. The material presented in this section of the Activity Book serves as a vehicle for the simultaneous teaching of science reading skills and science content.

The activities in this section are designed to help students develop specific science reading skills. The skills are organized into three general areas: comprehension skills, study skills, and vocabulary skills. The Science Gazette at the end of the textbook provides the content material for learning and practicing these reading skills. Each Science Gazette article has at least one corresponding science reading skill exercise.

Contents

Alan Kolata and Oswaldo Rivera: The Mysterious Canals of Bolivia

Science Reading Skill: Making Predictions

One of the most important and practical skills that can come from the study of science is the ability to make predictions. There is no mystery about making predictions. Although you may not realize it, every time you use a "hunch" or make a "guess" about what will happen in a certain situation, you are making a prediction. Reviewing questions that you believe will be on a test or taking an umbrella to school because you think it is going to rain are examples of making predictions.

The method used for making predictions involves applying what you already know to a set of conditions and thinking logically. When you read science material, use the same method. This exercise will help you sharpen your skill in making predictions.

A number of conditions are listed in Column A. In Column B are predictions based on these conditions. Select one condition from Column A that corresponds to each prediction in Column B. Write the numbers of your answers in the proper spaces on the chart.

Column A: Conditions

A. Kolata and Rivera needed to test their hypothesis.

B. A frost struck the area.

C. The crops in the channel were undamaged.

D. A mist lay over the floodplain.

E. The ancient peoples of this area learned how to protect their crops.

Column B: Predictions

1. Most of the hillside crops were lost.

2. The mist helped keep the crops warm.

3. They convinced one man to plant his potato crop in redug channels.

4. They had dug the channels.

5. The other farmers cooperated with the archaeologists.

A. Conditions	B. Predictions

Science Reading Skill: Defining Technical Words

Developing a vocabulary is a key to understanding what you read. You can expand your vocabulary by determining the meaning of a word, remembering that meaning, and using the word as often as you can. Sometimes the meaning of a word is made clear by its context, the way it is used in a sentence.

The following list of words is taken from this article. On the line to the right of each word, write its definition. Then on the line to the left of the word, indicate how you determined its meaning. Use the letter C if you figured out the meaning from the context, K if you already knew the meaning, and D if you had to look the word up in a dictionary.

_____ 1. depressions _____

_____ 2. inhabitants _____

_____ 3. succumbed _____

_____ 4. boggy _____

_____ 5. topographical _____

_____ 6. hypothesis _____

_____ 7. rejuvenate _____

_____ 8. archaeologists _____

_____ 9. capillary _____

_____ 10. bountiful _____

Now write a sentence of your own for each vocabulary word above.

11. _____

12. _____

13. _____

14. _____

15. _____

16. _____

17. _____

18. _____

19. _____

20. _____

Logging in the National Forests:
A Conflict of Interests
Science Reading Skill: Skimming for Details

Skimming is a valuable skill for getting a particular piece of information quickly. You skim when you look for a word in the dictionary, when you use a telephone directory, or when you read a timetable for a train. In each case, you are looking for one particular item and you ignore everything else.

When you need to find a specific answer to a question in the textbook, it is not necessary to reread the entire chapter. Instead, let your eyes pass quickly over the reading material while you look for the key words, or the most important ideas. Then look for such clues as a number, a capital letter, a date, an italicized or boldfaced word, or quotation marks.

Working with this article, practice the skill of skimming for details. Read each of the following questions. Then skim the article to find the answer. Write your answer on the lines provided.

1. Where is the location of the forest mentioned in this article? _____

_____

2. What is the name of the bird that is threatened by the cutting of forest trees? _____

_____

3. What kinds of trees does this bird make its nest in? _____

_____

4. What government agency declared this bird a threatened species? _____

   When did this occur? _____

5. How many jobs may be lost if strict limitations on logging are put into place? _____

_____

6. What is "New Forestry?" _____

_____

Science Reading Skill: Summarizing

Summarizing is a very useful skill. Summary writing will help you to (1) concentrate better as you read, (2) organize what you read, (3) sort out the important points you need to learn, and (4) remember key ideas.

The First Step Is to Learn How to Summarize

Summarizing is a form of note taking. Therefore, use a separate piece of paper in your notebook. Do not write in the textbook. Write the topic or science lesson, page assignment, and date at the top of the page. As you read each paragraph, look for the main idea and supporting details. Sometimes one main idea will be discussed in several paragraphs. In such a case, find the details that directly relate to the main idea within the paragraphs. At other times a major heading or subheading may express the main idea. After reading each paragraph, write the key phrases or main points in your own words.

The Second Step Is to Practice Summarizing

Summarizing as you read forces you to pay attention to finding important ideas. Relating facts and ideas to one another helps you to see the pattern in which material is organized. Using your own words to summarize important ideas makes it easier for you to remember what you read.

The Third Step Is to Apply Your Skill

The purpose of summarizing is to help you remember what you read. You will also have a set of notes for review. Summarizing will become a timesaver, and may also help you improve your grades.

Summarize the article about logging in the national forests. Note the title of the article and its pages. Write the number of the paragraph in the left column. Write the page on which the paragraph appears in the middle column. Write your notes in the right column. A sample to begin your summary has been done for you.

Summarizing Worksheet

Paragraph	Page	Summary
1	I158	The spotted owl lives in the Cascade Mountain Range. This bird, active at night, is the center of a controversy.

Science Reading Skill: Effective Writing

In studying science, your skill in writing assignments, reports, and answers to test questions is very important. The purpose of written work is to communicate information. There are several basic rules you should follow when doing a written exercise. (1) Have a good working knowledge of the subject you are writing about. (2) Use correct vocabulary and punctuation. This includes spelling, sentence structure, and paragraph form. (3) Use logical reasoning in developing ideas so that they supply the information required. (4) Choose a topic sentence that states your purpose or identifies the main idea. (5) Always support your ideas by using factual information. (6) Reread what you have written to make sure that it is meaningful and represents your own thoughts.

A question appears at the end of this article. Write a response to this question in two or three paragraphs. Apply the rules you have just learned to write an effective answer. Use a sheet of paper for your written work.

Cities Under the Sea
Science Reading Skill: Making a Sketch

A sketch is a teaching technique as well as a learning technique. It is a form of communication that is older than speech. A sketch shows an idea. A sketch also cuts down on the amount of space needed to present material, either in your notes or in a textbook. Think of the saying, "A picture is worth a thousand words."

In this activity you will try your skill at making a sketch. Remember, a sketch must have a sense of proportion. It must also be as close a reproduction of the described content information as possible. You are not expected to be a professional artist, but you should be able to convey a true representation of the ideas you read.

In this article, there is a description of the way a person would look when traveling under the sea. Carefully read the material and then make a sketch showing the type of dress, some background scenery, and the method of travel under the sea. Use the space below for your sketch.

Science Reading Skill: Clues to Discovery

In studying science, it is important to understand how scientists arrive at conclusions. Scientific discovery begins by asking a specific question. Conducting experiments and collecting data are the processes by which scientists reach conclusions. In the same way, you can decide if a conclusion is reasonable from the facts supplied in the reading material. Does the conclusion make sense? Look for the facts or ideas that provide evidence or support for the conclusion. Make sure a conclusion is based on a number of facts. The more facts that are given, the more reliable the conclusion.

The following statements represent conclusions. Based on your reading of this science article, indicate if you agree or disagree with each of the statements. Provide evidence to support your decision. Use the information that directly relates to the content of the article. Write your answers on the lines provided under each statement.

Agree/Disagree

_____ **1.** In the future, humans may be able to breathe under the sea with a "gill."

_____

_____

_____

_____

_____

_____ **2.** Undersea storms are a real danger to humans who may live under the sea in the future. _____

_____

_____

_____

_____

_____ **3.** Fish and seaweed will be important sources of food for people who live in undersea cities in the future.

_____

_____

_____

_____

_____

Answer Key

Adventures in Science

Making Predictions A. 2 B. 4 C. 1
D. 5 E. 3 **Defining Technical Words**
1. hollows, low places 2. people living in a
particular area 3. die 4. wet, spongy
5. having to do with the surface features of
an area 6. suggested solution to a problem
7. bring back to youthful strength
8. scientists who study ancient cultures 9. a
force that moves molecules in a liquid
10. plentiful

Issues in Science

Skimming for Details 1. The Cascade
Mountain Range in the Pacific Northwest
2. The northern spotted owl 3. Ancient
trees 4. The United States Fish and Wildlife
Service, early 1990s 5. 30,000 6. Method
of cutting that leaves some old trees standing
and some cut trees on the forest floor.
Summarizing Student answers will vary.
Effective Writing Check student papers for
correctness.

Futures in Science

Making a Sketch Answers will vary. Check
student sketches to make sure they represent
accurately the material presented in the
article. **Clues to Discovery** 1. Agree. The
article describes a "gill" that will enable
humans to breathe under water in the future.
2. Disagree. The "weather" is always calm
under the sea; no storms could occur.
3. Agree. Fish and seaweed will be farmed
under the sea. Actually, this occurs today
using methods slightly different from those
described in the article.

Activity Bank

TO THE TEACHER

One of the most exciting and enjoyable ways for students to learn science is for them to experience it firsthand—to be active participants in the investigative process. Throughout the *Prentice Hall Science* program, ample opportunity has been provided for hands-on, discovery learning. With the inclusion of the Activity Bank in this Activity Book, students have additional opportunities to hypothesize, experiment, observe, analyze, conclude, and apply—all in a nonthreatening setting using a variety of easily obtainable materials.

These highly visual activities have been designed to meet a number of common classroom situations. They accommodate a wide range of student abilities and interests. They reinforce and extend a variety of science skills and encourage problem solving, critical thinking, and discovery learning. The required materials make the activities easy to use in the classroom or at home. The design and simplicity of the activities make them particularly appropriate for ESL students. And finally, the format lends itself to use in cooperative-learning settings. Indeed, many of the activities identify a cooperative-learning strategy.

Students will find the activities that follow exciting, interesting, entertaining, and relevant to the science concepts being learned and to their daily lives. They will find themselves detectives, observing and exploring a range of scientific phenomena. As they sort through information in search of answers, they will be reminded to keep an open mind, ask lots of questions, and most importantly, have fun learning science.

Contents

Activity

Earth's Atmosphere

CHAPTER 1

A Model of Acid Rain

In many parts of the country, rain contains chemical pollutants that produce harmful effects. You may have read about acid rain. Acid rain can kill fishes in lakes and damage the leaves of trees. In cities, acid rain can damage statues and buildings. You can make a model of acid rain and observe some of the harmful effects acid rain produces.

Materials

3 saucers
3 pennies
vinegar
teaspoon

Procedure

1. Place one penny in each of the three saucers.
2. Place two teaspoons of water on the penny in the first saucer.
3. Place two teaspoons of vinegar on the penny in the second saucer. Leave the third penny alone.

4. Set the three saucers aside and observe the three pennies the next day. (You may want to cover the saucers with a piece of plastic wrap to keep the liquids from evaporating.)

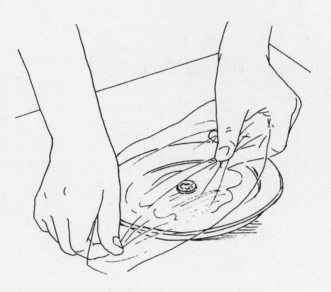

Observations

Describe the appearance of the three pennies. You may want to draw a picture of each penny.

_____

_____

Analysis and Conclusions

1. Explain the changes that occurred in the appearance of the three pennies.

_____

_____

_____

2. What do you think happens to rocks and other objects that are exposed to acid rain over a period of time?

_____

_____

_____

Going Further

With your classmates, see if you can devise a plan to protect the pennies from acid rain. Assume that you cannot stop acid rain from occurring. Present your ideas to your teacher before you test them out.

Activity   CHAPTER
                                                    Earth's Oceans **2**

Sink or Swim—Is It Easier to Float in Cold Water or Hot?

Can you float? You may already know that it is easier to float in salt water than in fresh water. Salt water is denser than fresh water. Is it easier to float in warm water or cold? Try this investigation to find out.

Materials
large, deep pan
cold tap water
hot tap water
food coloring
dropper bottle

Procedure
1. Fill a large pan three-quarters full of cold water.
2. Put a few drops of food coloring in a dropper bottle and fill the bottle with hot tap water. **CAUTION:** *Be careful not to scald yourself. The hot water from some taps is very hot indeed!*
3. Place your finger over the opening of the dropper bottle. Carefully place the bottle on its side in the pan of cold water. The dropper bottle should be submerged completely.
4. Slowly take your finger off the opening of the bottle. Observe what happens.

Food coloring

Exploring Planet Earth I ■ **183**

Observations

1. Describe what happened to the hot water.

_____

_____

_____

2. Why did you add food coloring to the hot water?

_____

_____

_____

Analysis and Conclusions

1. Which water, cold or hot, was more dense? Why?

_____

_____

_____

2. Which water, cold or hot, would be easier to float in? Why?

_____

_____

_____

Going Further

Suppose you had placed cold water and food coloring in the dropper bottle and hot water in the pan. What do you think would have happened when you removed your finger from the dropper bottle? With your teacher's permission, test your hypothesis.

 **A**ctivity _____ Earth's Fresh Water

How Does a Fish Move?

Fishes are well adapted for life in water. In this activity you will observe a fish and discover for yourself how fishes are suited to live in water.

Materials
small goldfish
aquarium
fish food
thermometer
watch or clock
several sheets of unlined paper

Procedure 🎥

1. On a sheet of unlined paper, draw an outline of the fish from the side. On the same sheet of paper, draw an outline of the fish as seen head-on. On the same sheet of paper, draw an outline of the fish as seen from the top.

2. As you observe your fish, draw its fins on your outlines. Use arrows to show how each fin moves. If a fin doesn't appear to move, indicate this on your drawing.

3. Feed the fish. Record its reaction to food.

4. Take the temperature of the water. Enter the temperature reading in the Data Table on the next page. Now count the number of times the fish opens and closes its gills in 1 minute. (The gills are located at the front end of the fish just behind its eyes. In order to live, fish take oxygen from the water. They swallow water through their mouth and pass it out through their gills.)

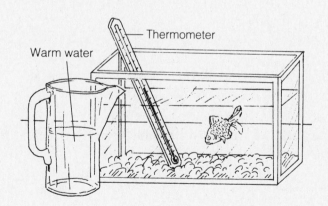

5. Add a little warm water to the aquarium. You want to raise the temperature of the water only a few degrees, so be careful. Do not make too drastic a change in the water temperature. Count the number of times the gills open and close in the warmer water in 1 minute. Record this information in the Data Table.

Observations

1. What fin or fins move the fish forward in the water?

_____

_____

2. What fins help the fish turn from side to side?

_____

_____

DATA TABLE

	Gills Open and Close
Temperature 1	
Temperature 2	

3. How does the movement of the gills relate to the temperature of the water?

_____

_____

Analysis and Conclusions

What special structures and behaviors enable fishes to survive in a water world?

_____

_____

_____

Going Further

You might like to set up an aquarium that reflects a fish's natural environment more accurately. For example, add a gravel layer to the bottom of the aquarium. Place some rocks and plants in the aquarium. You should then examine your fish's behavior after you have completed this task. What changes, if any, do you note?

ctivity   Earth's Fresh Water   CHAPTER **3**

What Is the Effect of Phosphates on Plant Growth?

Sometimes seemingly harmless chemicals have effects that are not easily predictable. For example, detergents are often added to water to clean clothes and dishes. When the clothes and dishes are rinsed, the detergents in waste water enter home septic systems or town sewage systems. Detergents in water may eventually be carried to streams, lakes, and sources of groundwater. So far this story seems unremarkable.

However, some detergents contain phosphates. Because of their effects on plant growth, detergents that contain phosphates have been banned by some communities. In this investigation you will measure the effects of phosphates on plant growth. You will uncover reasons why communities try to keep phosphates out of water supplies, and thus ban the use of certain detergents used to clean clothes and dishes.

Materials
2 large test tubes with corks or stoppers to fit
test-tube rack, or large plastic jar or beaker
2 sprigs of *Elodea*
detergent that contains phosphates
sunlight or a lamp
small scissors

Before You Begin
Make sure that the detergent you will be using contains phosphates; many do not. *Elodea* is a common water plant used in home aquariums. A local pet store is a good source of supply.

Procedure ⚗

1. Take two sprigs of *Elodea* and use your scissors to cut them to the same length. Do not cut the growing tip. Cut the opposite end. Measure the length of the sprigs and record the length in the Data Table on the next page. Place a sprig of *Elodea* into each test tube.

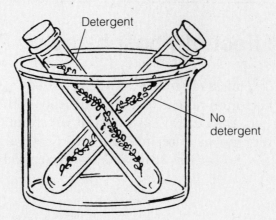

2. Add enough water to each test tube to fill it nearly to the top. Be sure the *Elodea* sprig is covered with water.

3. Place a small pinch of detergent into one test tube. Gently swirl the test tube to mix the water and detergent. Leave plain water in the other test tube.

4. Stopper each test tube.

5. Place the test tubes in a test-tube rack or plastic jar or beaker. Place the rack (or jar or beaker) in a sunny window or under another source of light.

6. Every three days for a month, carefully remove each *Elodea* sprig and measure it. Record your measurements in your data table. Place the sprigs back into the test tubes they were removed from each time. Do not mix up the sprigs!

Observations

1. What was the control in this experiment? Why?

_____

_____

2. Describe the *Elodea* that was placed in plain water.

_____

_____

3. Describe the *Elodea* that was placed in water that contained the detergent drops.

_____

_____

4. Why was it important to return each sprig to the correct tube?

_____

_____

Name _____ Class _____ Date _____

DATA TABLE

Day	Detergent	No Detergent
1		
4		
7		
10		
13		
16		
19		
22		
25		
28		
31		

Analysis and Conclusions

1. Did the detergent affect the *Elodea's* growth?

_____

_____

2. How do you explain the results of this investigation?

_____

_____

3. How might the effect of phosphates on water plants affect a community's water supply?

_____

_____

Going Further

Design an investigatation that compares the effects of detergents and fertilizers on plant growth. Have your teacher check the design of your investigation before you begin.

_A_ctivity _____ **Earth's Landmasses** CHAPTER **4**

Making Soil

Soil is a substance that is certainly taken for granted by most people. This common substance, often underfoot and easy to see, contributes greatly to human survival. Plants need soil to grow well—it is good, fertile soil that makes our croplands so productive. In this activity you will "make" some soil. Keep in mind, however, that what you can accomplish in an afternoon takes nature's forces many years to produce.

Materials
rocks
sand
magnifying glass
dried leaves
plastic pan or bucket
soil sample

Procedure
1. Use the magnifying glass to examine the rocks and the sand. Draw what you observe on a separate sheet of paper.

2. Place a thick layer of sand in the bottom of the plastic pan or bucket.

3. Break up the dried leaves into tiny pieces. You might even grind the dried leaves between two flat rocks.

4. Add a layer of the ground-up plant material to the sand. Use your hands to gently mix the sand and dried leaves together.

5. Use the magnifying glass to compare the soil mixture you made with the soil sample provided by your teacher. Draw what you observe.

Observations

1. How does the sand compare with the rock samples?

_____

_____

2. Did you observe leaves or other pieces of plant material in the soil sample provided by your teacher?

_____

_____

3. In what ways did the soil you made resemble the soil sample? In what ways was it different?

_____

_____

4. How could you make your soil more like the soil in the sample?

_____

_____

Analysis and Conclusions

1. Where does sand come from in natural soil?

_____

_____

2. Where does the plant material come from in natural soil?

_____

_____

3. Why is plant material an important part of soil?

_____

_____

4. Why are sand and other rock material important parts of soil?

_____

_____

Going Further

Design an experiment to compare the growth of plants in the soil you made with the growth of plants in natural soil. Discuss your plan with your teacher, and get his or her permission before you begin.

— **A**ctivity ———————————————————————— Earth's Interior — CHAPTER **5**

How Hard Is That Rock?

Hardness is a property that is often used to identify rocks. In this activity you will determine the hardness of several rock samples relative to each other and to several common substances. Geologists often use the Mohs hardness scale to determine the hardness of a rock specimen. But if you are collecting rocks in the field, it may not be easy to carry the ten mineral specimens that represent the Mohs hardness scale along with you. It is often easier to use commonly available substances to perform a hardness test.

For example, a fingernail has a hardness of about 2.5, a penny a hardness of 3.0, a steel knife blade a hardness of about 5.5, and a piece of glass a hardness of 5.5 to 6.0.

Materials
selection of rock samples
square glass plate
steel kitchen knife
penny

Procedure 🜔 ⚒

1. Select two rock specimens. Try to scratch one with the other. Keep the harder of the two specimens. Put the softer one aside.

2. Select another rock and use the same scratch test. Keep the harder of these two rocks and set the other aside.

3. Keep repeating the procedure until you have identified the hardest rock specimen you have.

4. Compare the rocks to find the second hardest rock. Continue this procedure until all the rock specimens have been put in order from the hardest to the softest.

5. Now compare the rock specimens to the other materials of known hardness to determine the actual hardness of as many of your specimens as possible. **CAUTION:** *Use care when handling sharp materials.* Your teacher will show you the proper way to proceed. Share your results with your classmates. Use their findings to confirm yours.

Observations

1. Did you find any rocks that were softer than your fingernail?

_____

_____

2. Did any rocks scratch the penny?

_____

_____

3. Were any rocks unscratched by the steel blade?

_____

_____

4. Did any rocks scratch the glass plate?

_____

_____

Analysis and Conclusions

1. Calcite has a rating of 3 on the Mohs scale. Would calcite be scratched by a penny?

_____

_____

_____

2. Many people think that diamond (10 on the Mohs scale) is the only mineral that can scratch glass. Is this correct? Why?

_____

_____

_____

Activity: A Model of Acid Rain

Observations The penny placed in plain water and the penny left alone will not change. The penny in the vinegar will begin to show color changes, usually a green film. **Analysis and Conclusions 1.** The penny that was covered with vinegar, an acid, began to turn green. The other pennies remained copper colored. Students actually made a model that shows the effects of acid rain on metal. **2.** Over time, acid rain will cause changes to occur in objects. Metals will corrode, statues made of stone will erode.

Activity: Sink or Swim—Is It Easier to Float in Cold Water or Hot?

Observations 1. The hot water moved upward in the pan of cold water. **2.** To make it easier to see. **Analysis and Conclusions 1.** Cold water is denser than hot water. The warm colored water moved up toward the surface of the cold water. **2.** The cold, denser water would be easier to float in. It would support a person's weight better than the less dense hot water. Actually the difference in density is very slight so there would probably be little, if any, difference in the ability of a person to float in water of either temperature.

Activity: How Does a Fish Move?

Observations 1. The tail fin is primarily used for forward motion. Other fins may cause the fish to move forward, too. **2.** The pectoral fins, located on the sides of the fish near the gills, turn the fish from side to side. The tail fin also can help the fish turn. **3.** The gills open and close more rapidly in warm water than in cold. **Analysis and Conclusions** Students should mention the gills that remove oxygen from, and give off carbon dioxide to, the water; and the fins that aid a fish in moving. Other answers are possible. For example, some students might mention the streamlined shape of fish, their protective scales, their colors.

Activity: What Is the Effect of Phosphates on Plant Growth?

Observations 1. Students were testing for the effects of detergent on plant growth, so the control was the plant that was placed in plain water. **2.** It increased in length. **3.** It should have shown a greater increase in length than the *Elodea* that was placed in plain water. **4.** It is important to place the sprigs back in the correct tubes so that the effects of the detergent on plant growth were confined to one plant. **Analysis and Conclusions 1.** Yes, the *Elodea* that was placed in the water that contained detergent showed greater growth. **2.** Phosphates in detergents act like plant fertilizers. Phosphates are used by plants as they grow. **3.** If large amounts of phosphates enter a community's water supply, plant growth in the water can increase rapidly. The increased number of plants may use all available nutrients and gases in the water. If this happens, the plants begin to die. The water becomes fouled. Fish and other organisms in the water may also die.

Activity: Making Soil

Observations 1. Sand particles are much smaller than the rock samples. Rocks break down into smaller and smaller particles during natural weathering processes that occur in nature. The smallest particles, consisting of compounds that made up the original rocks, are known as sand. Beach sand is a compound that is made of silicon and oxygen. **2.** Answers will vary depending upon the samples. Soil samples will contain plant material. **3.** Answers will vary depending upon the materials the students use. All samples should contain a mixture of material from nonliving (rocks and minerals) sources and plant materials.   **4.** Answers will vary, but students should suggest that better analysis of the components of the soil sample would result in soil more like the sample. **Analysis and Conclusions 1.** Sand results when rocks are broken down into very small particles.   **2.** The plant material in soil comes from plants that have died and decayed. Students might suggest falling leaves or soil additives such as peat moss as sources of plant material.   **3.** Decaying plant material supplies nutrients that enhance the growth of other plants. Decaying plant materials can be considered a kind of "natural" fertilizer. **4.** Sand and rock material improve soil drainage and porosity.

Activity: How Hard Is That Rock?

Observations Answers will vary depending upon the rock specimens that were available to students.   **Analysis and Conclusions 1.** No, it would not.   **2.** No, it is not correct. Diamond has a hardness of 10, glass has a hardness of 5.5 to 6.0. Any rock with a hardness greater than 6 will scratch glass.